The Coding Experts

CPC Practice Exam 2022

Complete Practice Exam for 600 Quesions & answers

Vinay Trivedi

You are Special

Contents

About the Author

Acknowledgment

Preface

About CPC Exam Changes

The CPC Exam New Breakdown

Tips for CPC Exam

Exam – 1 ....100 QUESTION EXAM

Exam - 2 ....100 QUESTION EXAM

Exam - 3 ....100 QUESTION EXAM

Exam - 4 ....100 QUESTION EXAM

Exam - 5 ....100 QUESTION EXAM

Exam - 6 ....100 QUESTION EXAM

Exam - 7 ....100 QUESTION EXAM

Answers

About the Author

Vinay Trivedi has been writing since childhood, when his mother gave him a lined notebook in which to write down his stories. (Much later, when Vinay thanked her for being the spark that ignited his writing career, she revealed that she'd given him the notebook to keep him quiet, "because every mom needs a break now and then.")

Vinay Trivedi want everyone to be success and that's why these books are written all for you people.

Acknowledgements

This work would not have been possible without the support of knowledge and dedication towards work.

I am grateful to all of those with whom I have had the pleasure to work during this and other related projects.

Nobody has been more important to me in the pursuit of this project than the members of my family. I would like to thank my parents, whose love and guidance are with me in whatever I pursue. They are the ultimate role models. Most importantly, I wish to thank my loving and supportive fiancée, Naina Yadav, who provide unending inspiration

Preface

This book is for the students who want a good career in US healthcare industry.

If you are preparing for AAPC CPC EXAM, this book contains the AAPC CPC practice exam which makes you understand the type of question in your real exam and how to solve them in a timely manner.

This Book is dedicated to all the CPC Students.

About CPC Exam

Starting January 1, 2022, AAPC certification exams will consist of 100 questions in which you'll be given 4 hours to answer.

To pass the CPC exam, you need to achieve a passing rate of 70 percent or higher. That means you must answer at least 70 questions correctly.

The CPC Exam Breakdown

Passing the CPC exam requires you to correctly answer a minimum of 70 questions from the series below. The exam questions, however, will not be identified or sorted by the series to which they pertain. The CPC test will rely on a level of understanding that enables you to identify the series.

10,000 Series CPT®

The 10,000 Series CPT® part of the exam will consists of six questions related to surgical procedures performed on the integumentary system, which includes skin, subcutaneous, and accessory structures, as well as nails, pilonidal cysts, repairs, destruction, and breast.

20,000 Series CPT®

The six questions in the 20000 Series CPT® will home in on surgical procedures performed on the musculoskeletal system from head to toe. Specifically, these areas include the head, neck, back and flank, spine, abdomen, shoulder, arm, hand and fingers, pelvis and hip, leg, foot and toes.

30,000 Series CPT®

Six questions covering the 30000 Series CPT® focus on surgical procedures performed on the respiratory system, surgical procedures performed on the cardiovascular system, surgical procedures performed on the hemic and lymphatic systems, and surgical procedures performed on the mediastinum and diaphragm.

40,000 Series CPT®

Your knowledge of the 40000 Series CPT® will be tested with six questions targeting surgical procedures performed on the digestive system, which will focus on these areas: lips, mouth, palate and uvula, salivary gland and ducts, pharynx, adenoids, and tonsils, esophagus, stomach, intestines, appendix, rectum, anus, liver, biliary tract, pancreas, abdomen, peritoneum, and omentum.

50,000 Series CPT®

The CPC exam will assess your knowledge of the 50000 Series CPT® with six questions pertaining to surgical procedures performed on the urinary system, surgical procedures performed on the male reproductive system, surgical procedures performed on the female reproductive system, including maternity and delivery, and surgical procedures performed on the endocrine system.

60,000 Series CPT®

Six questions directed at the 60000 Series® involve surgical procedures performed on the nervous system and will include codes pertaining to the skull, meninges, brain, spine, spinal cord, extracranial nerves, peripheral nerves, autonomic nervous system.

Evaluation and Management

Six E/M questions will assess your coding proficiency related to place and level of services, such as office/other outpatient, hospital observation, hospital inpatient, consultations, emergency department, critical care, nursing facility, domiciliary and rest homes, and home services. It will also include questions directed at preventive medicine, non-face-to-face services, neonatal and pediatric critical care, intensive care, prolonged services, chronic care, transitional care, case management, and care plan oversight.

Anesthesia

Four questions related to anesthesia will pertain to time reporting, qualifying circumstances, physical status modifiers, anesthesia for surgical, diagnostic and obstetric services.

Radiology

The six questions in this section of the CPC test will focus on both diagnostic and interventional radiology, including diagnostic ultrasound, radiologic guidance, mammography, bone and joint studies, radiation oncology, and nuclear medicine.

Laboratory / Pathology

Six path/lab questions will determine your knowledge of organ and disease panels, drug testing, therapeutic drug assays, evocation/suppression testing, consultations, urinalysis, molecular pathology, MAAA, chemistry, hematology and coagulation, immunology, transfusions, microbiology, anatomic pathology, cytopathology, cytogenetic studies, surgical pathology, in vivo and reproductive.

Medicine

Six questions will cover numerous specialty-specific coding scenarios, as well as immunizations, biofeedback, dialysis, central nervous system assessments, health and behavior assessments, hydration, medical nutrition, therapeutic and diagnostic administration, chemotherapy administration, photodynamic therapy, osteopathic manipulative treatment, patient education and training, non-face-to-face nonphysician services, and moderate sedation.

Medical Terminology

Medical terminology for all systems in the human body will be assessed in four questions.

Anatomy

Anatomy for all systems in the human body will be assessed in four questions.

ICD-10-CM/Diagnosis

Five questions will require proficiency in diagnosis for all the chapters included in ICD-10-CM, as well as thorough knowledge of the ICD-10-CM Official Guidelines for Coding and Reporting. Additionally, diagnosis questions will appear in other sections of the exam from the CPT® categories.

Hcpcs Level 2

Three questions on the CPC exam will pertain to HCPCS Level II coding and include questions focusing on modifiers, supplies, medications, and professional services for Medicare patients.

Coding Guidelines

This section of the CPC test will involve seven questions addressing the ICD-10-CM Official Guidelines for Coding and Reporting, CPT® coding guidelines and parenthetical notes, and modifier use.

Compliance and Regulatory

Three questions testing your knowledge of compliance and regulations will pertain to services covered under Medicare Parts A, B, C and D; applying coding to payment policy, place of service reporting, fraud and abuse, NCCI edits, NCD/LCD, HIPAA, ABNs, and RVUs.

(Note: New Section) Cases

Ten cases with one multiple choice question per case will test your ability to accurately code medical record documentation using CPT®, ICD-10-CM, and HCPCS Level II. The cases will cover 10000 series, 20000 series, 30000 series, 40000 series, 50000 series, 60000 series, medicine, anesthesia, radiology, pathology and laboratory, and evaluation and management services. Medical terminology, anatomy, compliance, and regulatory information may also be tested in the cases.

Tips for CPC Exam

It is all about the guidelines: In preparation for the exam, review all coding guidelines and understand how they are applied. This pertains to all codebooks (CPT®, ICD-10-CM, HCPCS Level II). Coding conventions and guidelines for ICD-10-CM are found in the front of the codebook. CPT® guidelines are found in the introductory sections and throughout the codebook in selected subsections.

Get your materials organized: Well-marked codebooks can be extremely helpful during the exam. Because coding guidelines contain instructions for what can be reported and what cannot be reported, use different colored highlighters to quickly distinguish between the two.

Sequencing matters: Follow sequencing rules in coding guidelines and coding conventions. Example: A urine culture confirms the patient's diagnosis of a UTI caused by E. coli. The correct codes and sequence are: 599.0, 041.49. There is a note instructing you to use an additional code to identify the organism, such as Escherichia coli (E. coli). If there are code options with the same codes in a different sequence, pay close attention to the coding conventions and guidelines to guide you in the right selection.

Parenthetical notes provide valuable information: Paying close attention to information in the CPT® parenthetical notes prevents you from making coding errors. Example: There is a parenthetical note following code 10030 which states "Do not report 10030 in conjunction with 75989, 76942, 77002, 77003, 77012, 77021. This alerts the coder that imaging guidance cannot be reported with the surgical procedure code.

Know your modifiers: Review the proper use for each modifier. Understand when each should be appended.

Example: Modifier 26 is appended to codes with a professional and technical component to indicate the provider you are coding for only performed the professional component. If the question/scenario indicates the procedure is performed in the hospital setting, the coder will be alerted that modifier 26 should be appended to radiology procedures and medicine procedures that apply. If the code description includes professional component (e.g. 93010), you would not append modifier 26.

Exam - 1

Integumentary System (10000 Series)

1. Dr. John, a plastic surgeon completed a bilateral rhytidectomy of the neck and a suction assisted lipectomy of the right upper arm. What codes should be reported for Dr. John's services?

a. 15828-50, 15879-RT-59

b. 15826-59, 15879-RT-59

c. 15828-50, 15879-RT-59

d. 15826-RT, 15828-50, 15878-RT-59

2. Roger had a dermal lesion on his left foot. The physician completed a punch biopsy and then removed the lesion by shaving during the same session. The lesion diameter was documented as 3.6 cm. The defect was covered by a sterile dressing. Roger was instructed to follow-up in 3 days. What codes should the physician use to report these services?

a. 11308-LT

b. 11308-LT, 11104-59

c. 11303-LT

d. 11424-LT, 11104-59

3. Dr. Long completed an excision of a malignant lesion from the scalp of a 45-year-old patient. The patient was prepped and draped in the usual sterile fashion and Lidocaine locally injected. Dr. Long documented the size of the lesion as 2.0 cm. The lesion was excised and marked at the 12 o'clock cephalad portion with a silk suture. The total excised diameter of lesion and margins was 4.0 cm. The defect created by the excision was 5.4 cm and closed with layer 3-0 Prolene sutures. How should Dr. Long report her services?

a. 11624, 12032-51, 96372, J2001

b. 11624, 12032-51

c. 11422, 12032-51, 96372, J2001

d. 11626, 12032-51

4. A 61-year-old patient had a benign 1-cm lesion excised from his right arm, a benign 2.5-cm lesion excised from his trunk, and a benign 2.1-cm lesion excided from his neck. The final excised diameters were documented at 1.9 cm right arm, 3.1 cm trunk, and 2.0 cm neck. The defect created on the arm by the excision was 2.8 cm, defect trunk 3.8 cm, and neck 2.8 cm. All defects were closed by simple suture technique. How should you report these services?

a. 11422, 11404-59, 11402-RT-59

b. 11422, 12004-51, 11404-59, 11402-59

c. 11401, 11403-51, 11423-51

d. 11602-RT, 11604-59, 11622-59

5. A patient has a pressure ulcer on his left ischial tuberosity. After examination a decision is made to complete debridement. The documented area debrided is 32 sq cm, including muscle and subcutaneous tissue. How should you report this service?

a. 97597-LT, 97598-LT-51

b. 11044-LT, 11047-LT-51
c. 11043-LT, 11046-LT
d. 11043-LT, 11046-LT, 97597-LT-59, 97598-LT-51

6. Amy, a 45-year-old patient, was scheduled for a biopsy following a diagnostic mammogram that showed a mass in the right breast. Dr. Tapper completed a percutaneous automated vacuum assisted biopsy and placement of a percutaneous localized clip in the right breast under ultrasonic guidance. The biopsy revealed a primary neoplasm of the lower-outer quadrant. How should you report Dr. Tapper's professional services?

a. 19085, 76942-26   b. 19081

c. 19083-26, 76942-26   d. 19083

Musculoskeletal System (20000 Series)

7. Jack fell from a ladder, six months ago, and broke his left radius. The fracture is not healing as expected and the implant needs to be replaced. Today, Jack underwent a secondary procedure. Dr. Gene completed an open treatment with internal fixation of the radial neck, including replacement of the prosthetic radial head. How

should you report Dr. Gene's services?

a. 24666-LT

b. 24366-LT

c. 25607-LT

d. 24587-LT

8. A patient, under general anesthesia, underwent a primary repair to the left ankle for a disrupted ligament. During the same procedure the patient required a percutaneous tenotomy to lengthen the Achilles tendon. How should you report the surgeon's services?

a. 27695-LT, 27606-59-LT

b. 27698-LT, 27685-59-LT, 01472-47

c. 27695-LT, 27685-59-LT, 01472-47

d. 27698-LT, 27605-59-LT

9. Dr. Hewes completed an anterior arthrodesis fusion, with a structural allograft, and minimal discectomy at L1-2, L3-4, and L4-5. Anterior instrumentation was required and inserted for stabilization of the entire lumbar region. How should Dr. Hewes' report this procedure?

a. 22612, 22614 x 2, 20931, 22846

b. 22558, 22585 x 2, 20931, 22846

c. 22558, 22585 x 2, 20931-51, 22846-62

d. 63075, 22558, 22614 x 2, 20931-51, 22846-62

10. A patient is stabbed in the right arm. The stab wound is enlarged, cleaned, and foreign materials removed and inspected, and coagulation of minor blood vessels is completed. What code(s) should you report for this service?

a. 20103, 24200

b. 20103

c. 24200, 24000-59

d. 24000, 20103-59

11. A 62-year-old female patient is referred to Dr. Stegman for increased right groin pain. The patient describes the pain as worse when sitting and rising from a seated position. The pain is temporarily relieved with intra articular corticosteroid injections. Monday, Dr. Stegman's physical examination documents loss of hip internal rotation, suspected cam lesion, and referral for x-ray with arthrography followed by CT with contrast. Both the x-ray and CT scan verify a cam lesion. Today, one week after the initial consult, Dr. Stegman completed a surgical right hip arthroscopy, including a femoroplasty to repair the cam lesion. How should Dr. Stegman report today's services?

a. 29860-RT, 73525-26, 73701-26

b. 29914-RT, 73525, 73701

c. 29914-RT

d. 27130-RT

12. Which is the correct CPT definition of external fixation?

a. The usage of skeletal pins plus an attaching mechanism/device used for tempora or definitive treatment of acute or chronic bony deformity.

b. The usage of skin application for force by an attaching mechanism/device used for permanent or definitive treatment of acute bone deformity.

c. The usage of skeletal pins plus an attaching mechanism/device used for permanent or definitive treatment of chronic bony deformity.

d. The usage of skin and skeletal pins plus an application of mechanism/device used for temporary treatment of acute or chronic bony deformity.

Respiratory And Cariovascular Systems (30000 Series)

13. A 20-year-old smoker has a single 8.2-mm lung nodule reported on CT of the chest. The peripheral nodule is not amendable to biopsy by routine bronschoscopy. The patient agreed to undergo a diagnostic bronchoscopy with computer-assisted navigation under moderate sedation. Dr. Smith completed the procedure and provided moderate sedation with a trained observer. The intra-service time was documented as 45 minutes. How should Dr. Smith report her codes for this procedure?

a. 31622, 31627

b. 31622, 31627-51

c. 31622, 31627-51, 76376, 99152, 99153

d. 31622, 31627, 99152, 99153

14. A patient with a benign neoplasm of the bronchus and lung underwent a bronchoplasty with a cartilage autograft repair. The thoracotomy site was closed with layered closure and a chest tube left in place for drainage. How should you report this procedure and diagnosis?

a. D14.30, 31770

b. C80.1, D14.30, 31775, 20910-51

c. D3A.090, 31825

d. D14.30, D3A.090, 31775, 31825-51

15. A 22-year-old patient who suffers from severe persistent asthma underwent a flexible bronschoscopy with bronchial thermoplasty in the right middle lobes. Dr. Aster's nurse, who is a trained independent observer, monitored the patient during the 45-minute intra-service time. Dr. Aster completed the procedure and administered moderate conscious sedation. How should Dr. Aster report this procedure?

a. 31661, 99152, 99153

b. 31661

c. 31622, 31661-51, 99152, 99153-51

d. 31645, 31661-51, 99152, 99153-51

16. Darlene underwent (SRS/SRBT) thoracic target delineation for sterotactic body radiation therapy. Her course of treatment required four sessions. How should the surgeon report this procedure?

a. 31626, 32701 x 4

b. 32701, 77435

c. 32701 x 4

d. 32701

17. Harry, a neonate weighing 3 kg, underwent a complex aortic valvuloplasty with cardiopulmonary bypass using transventricular dilation. During the same operative session a transmyocardial laser revascularization by thoracotomy was completed. How should you report this procedure?

a. 33140, 33141

b. 33390, 33141

c. 33391, 33141

d. 33140, 33390, 33141-51

18. Martin, a 54-year-old patient, underwent an insertion of a permanent pacemaker with transvenous electrodes placed in the right atrium and ventricle. The pacemaker device was evaluated and then placed in a subcutaneous pocket just below the ribcage. Dr. Gary completed this procedure, for Martin, under moderate conscious sedation and used fluoroscopic guidance to confirm lead placement. How should Dr. Gary report his professional services?

a. 33208

b. 33208, 76000-26, 93279-51

c. 33217, 33213-51

d. 33211, 76000-26, 93279-51

Digestive System (40000 Series)

19. A 26-year-old male patient had abnormal anal cytology on a screening exam. Today, the patient underwent a high-resolution anoscopy with four biopsies. How should you report today's service?

a. 46606

b. 46607

c. 46600, 46606 x 4

d. 46600, 46601, 46607 x 4

20. A 45-year-old male patient suffers from postprandial chest pain and abdominal pain. After workup and testing, he is diagnosed with a large paraesophageal hernia. Today, he undergoes a laparoscopic repair with implantation of mesh and a wedge gastroplasty. How

should you report today's service?

a. 43282, 43283

b. 43281, 43282, 43283

c. 43332, 43283-51

d. 43280, 43283

21. Dr. Singh documents that a 57-year-old female patient presented to the office with rectal bleeding and watery diarrhea. The patient states these conditions have been ongoing for the past two weeks. The patient indicates she had noticed occasional rectal bleeding prior to the diarrhea. After clinical and diagnostic studies, Dr. Singh confirms a large tumor of the posterior rectal wall with the lower margin 5 cm from the anal verge. The patient undergoes a transanal full-thickness excision of the tumor. How should Dr. Singh report the procedure?

a. 45172, 0184T-59

b. 45190

c. 45172

d. 45160

22. A 61-year-old male patient has an unresectable carcinoma in the head of the pancreas. The patient agrees with treatment and undergoes the following procedure in the hospital. Dr. Cohn placed the patient under moderate sedation and then completed percutaneous placement of interstitial fiducial marker utilizing fluoroscopic guidance for visualization and confirmation of marker position. The patient was under sedation and for one hour as an independent observer monitored the patient's consciousness and physiological status. How should Dr. Cohn's report his professional services for this procedure?

a. 49411, 99152, 99153 x 2, 77002-26

b. 49411, 77002-26

c. 99152, 49411-59, 77002-26

d. 49411, 49412-51, 99156, 99157 x 2, 77002-26

23. Dr. Sanchez completed a harvest and transfer for an extra abdominal omental flap procedure for correction of chest wall defect in an 8-year-old patient. How should Dr. Sanchez report his procedure?

a. 49904

b. 44700, 49905

c. 49904, 20920-59

d. 44700, 49904-62, 20920-59

24. What codes should you report with the add-on code 49568?

a. 11004-11006

b. 49560-49566

c. Both A and B

d. None of the above

Genitourinary System (50000 Series)

25. A patient underwent a complex cystometogram with bladder voiding pressure study and a urethral EMG. What codes should you use to report these services?

a. 51728, 51784-51

b. 51725, 51785-51
c. 51726, 51797-59
d. 51728, 51784-59

26. A 34-year-old patient gave birth to her third child via a cesarean delivery following an attempted vaginal delivery. Her two previous deliveries were vaginal without complications. She requested a tubal ligation be completed at the time of delivery. Dr. Milton followed this patient from the time of conception providing antepartum care, completed the delivery with tubal ligation, and will follow the patient through postpartum care. How should Dr. Milton report her services for this patient?

a. 59510, 58611

b. 59618, 58611

c. 59510, 58605-59

d. 59618, 58611-59

27. Lydia, a 25-year-old patient, was self-referred to Dr. Nedder for further examination and testing due to findings of severe dysplasia on her previous pap smear. Today, at the first visit with Dr. Nedder, he documented a comprehensive history, comprehensive examination, and moderate decision-making. He then performed a colposcopic examination with three biopsies of the cervix, endocervical curettage, and endometrial sampling. How should Dr. Nedder report his services?

a. 99213-25, 57455, 57456, 58110

b. 99244-25, 57454, 58110

c. 99204-25, 57454, 58110

d. 99204-25, 57455, 57456, 58110

28. Sandy, a 46-year-old patient, underwent anterior colporrhaphy, repair of a cystocele with repair of the urethrocele and inserted mesh. The procedure was completed via a vaginal approach. How should you report this surgery?

a. 57240, 57267

b. 57250, 57267

c. 57240, 57267-51

d. 57240, 49568-51

29. A patient underwent a surgical laparoscopy with ablation of four renal lesions. The surgeon used ultrasound guidance during the procedure. How should you report this service?

a. 50205, 77002-26

b. 50542

c. 50593

d. 50542, 77002-26

30. Jeannie, a 28-year-old female patient presented to the office with a concern that her IUD was "lost internally." Upon examination in the office, an attempt was made to remove the IUD but due to discomfort, the procedure was stopped. The next morning, Jeannie was taken to the outpatient surgical center and the IUD was removed, without complication, under general anesthesia. There was active bleeding at the end of the procedure. The patient tolerated the procedure well and was taken to recovery. How should Dr. Minor report the removal of the IUD?

a. 58300, 58301-59

b. 58301

c. 00840-P1, 58301

d. 58301-47

Endocrine, Nervous System, Eye And Ear (60000 Series)

31. A patient with hydrocephalus required an aspiration and investigative nonvascular shuntogram completed via a puncture into a previously placed shunt to check for effective drainage. This procedure was completed in the emergency room. How should you report the physician's professional services for this procedure?

a. 61070, 75809-26

b. 62180, 75898-26

c. 62220, 75809-26

d. 62160, 75898-26

32. Which of the following statement(s) is correct when reporting cranial stereotactic radiosurgery?

a. Report code 61796 when all lesions are simple

b. Report code 61798 if treating multiple lesions and any single lesion treated is complex.

c. Do not report codes 61796-61800 in conjunction with code 20660.

d. All of the above.

33. With which code set or individual codes can add-on code 61781 be correctly reported?

a. 61720-61791

b. 62201 or 77432

c. 77371-77373

d. None of the above

34. Dr. Tubman completed and excision and repair to one-half of the margin of the left eyelid on Logan, a 42-year-old patient. During this procedure, Dr. Tubman completed preparation for skin grafts. Logan will undergo graft procedure when the lid margin is evaluated for proper healing. How should Dr. Tubman report her services?

a. 67950-LT

b. 67971-LT, 15120-59

c. 67966-LT, 15120=59

d. 67966-LT

35. Dr. Grant injected Mrs. Brown with two units of chemodenervation (Onabotulinumtoxin A) to treat her bilateral blepharospasm. How should Dr. Grant report his services?

a. 67345-50, J0585x2

b. 67345

c. 64612-50, J0585x2

d. 64612

36. Following an accident, a patient underwent a removal of the lens in his right eye via a pars plana approach without a vitrectomy. A McCannel suture technique was used to repair the ciliary body at the end of the procedure. How should you report these services?
a. 66982-50, 66250-RT-59
b. 66852-RT, 66682-RT-51
c. 66840-E3, 66250-E3-59
d. 66820, 66682-51, 66990-51

Evaluation And Management

37. Discharge note: Dr. Kara dictated and completed service.

Mr. Davis, a 54-year-old male patient, is doing well following laparoscopic appendectomy completed at Calvin Hospital yesterday. He has been afebrile since the procedure, tolerating surgical soft diet, and ambulating with minimal assistance. He states he has "quality help" at home with his wife and son. Given his current improved condition and eagerness to leave the hospital, he will be discharged today. The nursing staff will provide discharge instructions and review these with the patient and home health team (family). A follow-up office visit is set for 10 days. I have instructed the patient to notify me immediately if he experiences a fever, pain, or oozing from the operative site. How should Dr. Kara report today's service?

a. 99232-25, 99239

b. 99238

c. 99315

d. 99232-25, 99217

38. Dr. Martin admitted Mrs. Worth to Community Hospital for a laparoscopic cholecystectomy and cholangiograms. Dr. Martin's admission was documented as a comprehensive history, comprehensive examination, and moderate decision-making. Later that same day (10 hours later), after tolerating the procedures well, Mrs. Worth was discharged without complications. She was instructed to call Dr. Martin if she experienced any problems. Mrs. Worth's sister accompanied her home and will be her primary caregiver for the next few days. Mrs. Worth was instructed to call Dr. Martin's office and schedule a follow- up visit. How should Dr. Martin report her services for the admission?

a. 99222, 99238

b. 99225

c. 99235

d. 99219, 99217

39. What code range should you use if the same physician provides critical care services to a neonate or a pediatric patient in both the outpatient and inpatient settings on the same day?

a. 99460-99463

b. 99291-99292

c. 99468-99476

d. 99281-99285

40. Baby-boy Busch was evaluated in the birthing centre the morning of his birth. The documentation noted a comprehensive examination and a maternal/fetal/and newborn history, and decision making for discharge was straight-forward. Documentation revealed a normal newborn and decision was made to discharge later on the same day. Bow should you report this service?
a. 99463
b. 99460-25, 99463
c. 99221-25, 99238
d. 99234

41. Dr. South documented a comprehensive history, comprehensive examination, and high complexity decision making for this first visit with Burton, a 19-year-old patient. Burton has a complicated history of diabetes mellitus, which continues to be out of control, further complicated with current alcohol and drug abuse. Additionally, Burton brought tests results that he received three days ago from his visit

to a free clinic. These test results were positive for a sexually transmitted disease. Dr. South spent two hours face-to-face talking with Burton. How should Dr. South report her services for today?

a. 99354-25, 99355

b. 99245, 99356

c. 99205, 99354

d. 99215, 99354-51, 99355-51

42. Danielle, a 39-year-old established patient, was seen for her annual female examination. Documentation was completed related to a comprehensive female exam, including discussion of current birth control pills and a prescription for refill for the following year. During this visit, Danielle showed Dr. Bill a growth on her right arm. Dr. Bill completed a separate workup, including documentation of a problem-focused examination and straightforward medical decision-making. Dr. Bill completed an incisional biopsy of the lesion and noted a suspected benign lesion. Dr. Bill told Danielle that she would get a call with results from the biopsy the next day. Additionally, Dr. Bill instructed Danielle to watch the growth on her arm and to schedule a follow-up visit for reevaluation if any changes should occur. How should Dr. Bill report today's services?

a. 99395, 11106-57

b. 99213-25, 99385, 11106-57

c. 99214, 99395-25, 11106-25

d. 99395, 99212-25, 11106

Anesthesia (00000 Series)

43. Dr. Sally, an anesthesiologist, provided general anesthesia for a 72-year-old patient with mild hypertension undergoing an open arthroscopy of the humeral neck. During this procedure, Dr. Sally was not supervising or monitoring any other cases. How should Dr. Sally report her codes for this case?

a. 01630-AA-P2, 99100

b. 01620-AA-P2, 99100

c. 01630-P2

d. 01634-P2

44. James, a 74-year-old patient who has severe hypertension that is difficult to manage, cut his lower right leg while water skiing. He suffered a deep open wound of the right lower leg with exposed fibula due to the injury. He underwent an emergency muscle flap repair with grafts from his right thigh to the right lower leg to repair the open defect. This case required general endotracheal anesthesia with medical

necessity for both an anesthesiologist and an independently acting CRNA. What anesthesia codes should Dr. Smith, the anesthesiologist, and Jane, the CRNA, report?

a. Dr. Smith: 01480-P3, 99100, 99140-51; Jane: 01480-P3, 99100, 99140-51

b. Dr. Smith: 01470-QZ-P3, 99100-51; Jane: 01470-AA-P3, 99100-51

c. Dr. Smith: 01480-AA-P3, 99100, 99140; Jane: 01480-QZ-P3, 99100, 99140

d. Dr. Smith: 01470-AA-P3, 99100, 99140; Jane: 01470-QZ-P3, 99100, 99140

45. Mark, a 45-year-old, mild diabetic patient, underwent an abdominal radical orchiectomy. Dr. Terry, the anesthesiologist, administered general anesthesia and an epidural infusion for control and management of postoperative pain. What codes should Dr. Terry report for this case?

a. 00928-51, 62322-P1

b. 00928-51, 62322-59

c. 00926-AA-P1

d. 00920-AA-59

46. Code 00940, anesthesia for vaginal procedures, has a base value of three (3) units. The patient was admitted under emergency circumstances, qualifying circumstance code 99140, which allows two (2) extra base units. A pre-anesthesia assessment was performed and signed at 2:00 a.m. Anesthesia start time is reported as 2:21 am, and the surgery began at 2:28 am. The surgery finished at 3:25 am and the patient was turned over to PACU at 3:36 am, which was reported as the ending anesthesia time. Using fifteen-minute time increments

and a conversion factor of $100, what is the correct anesthesia charge?

a. $ 800.00

b. $900.00

c. $1,000.00

d. $1,200.00

Radiology (70000)

47. Jane, a 45-year-old asymptomatic female patient completed an annual screening mammogram on Monday, revealing a mass in the left breast. After reading the screening mammogram, the radiologist on Tuesday scheduled the patient for follow-up unilateral diagnostic mammogram with computer aided detection. The diagnostic mammogram showed a primary neoplasm of the lower outer quadrant. How should the radiologist report his professional services for Tuesday?

a. 77065-26-LT

b. 77067-26-50, 77065-26-LT

c. 77065-26-RT

d. 77066-26-LT

48. Dr. Levitt's office owns and operates the x-ray equipment he used to complete the reading of the films for this patient. At the conclusion of the x-ray and his interpretation, he dictated the following report:

Patient: Mrs. Russell
X-ray left foot: Three views

Impressions: Fracture of distal phalanx, first digit Fractures of second and third digits (phalangeal). There is a fracture of the proximal portion of the first-digit phalanx. A comminuted fracture is noted in the middle phalanx of the second digit and an increased density is seen medially in the joint space of the middle phalanx of the third and fourth digits. Oblique films confirm displaced fragment of bone between the second and third digits. No other abnormalities present or noted. How should Dr. Levitt report his services?

a. 73630-LT

b. 73620-26-LT

c. 73650-LT

d. 73630-26-LT

49. A patient with a diagnosis of primary hyperparathyroidism underwent a parathyroid planar imaging with SPECT and concurrently acquired CT. How should you report this study and the diagnosis?

a. 78070, 70498, 78071, E21.0

b. 78072, E21.3

c. 78803, 78099, 78071, E21.0

d. 78072, E21.0

50. Ralph is a 52-year-old male undergoing treatment for a malignant tumor in his right lung. On Monday, he received his regularly scheduled radiation treatment with 10 MeV to a single treatment area. Today, on Wednesday, he received intracavitary hyperthermia treatment. How should you report Wednesday's service?

a. 77620

b. 77600

c. 77620, 77402

d. 77605, 77402-26

51. A patient underwent a thyroid imaging test with vascular flow and three uptakes on the same date of service. How would you report this study?

a. 78014x3

b. 78014

c. 78012, 78014x3

d. 78015, 78020x3

52. A patient underwent a single planar stress cardiac blood pool imaging study with gated equilibrium, wall motion and ejection fraction. In addition to the primary blood pool study, a first-pass technique at rest with right ventricular ejection fraction was completed. How should you report this service?

a. 78473, 78496

b. 78472, 78496

c. 78472, 78452, 78496

d. 78481, 78483

Pathology And Laboratory (80000 Series)

53. Brent, a 37-year-old patient, had a comprehensive metabolic panel completed. In addition to the comprehensive metabolic panel, from the same single collection, a renal function panel was completed. How should you report these services?

a. 80053-22

b. 80069, 82247, 84075, 84155, 84460, 84450

c. 80053, 80069

d. 80053, 84100

54. Jason, a 17-year-old patient, arrived at the ER after taking drugs and drinking. He was semiconscious and told the ER staff that he took his cousin's Phenobarbital and another pill he could not identify. The laboratory completed a therapeutic assay for Phenobarbital, multiple drug class testing utilizing two nonchromatographic methods, and three confirmation procedures. How should you report the drug screening and confirmation in this case?

a. 80184, 80305

b. 80305 x2, 80184 x3

c. 80305, 80306, 80307

d. 80184, 80307

55. Patient required a C-section delivery during her early second trimester. Her placenta was submitted for gross and microscopic pathology examination following the C-section delivery. The placenta was submitted in two separate specimens and a decalcification procedure was utilized during pathology testing. How should you report this pathology service?

a. 88307 x 2, 88111

b. 88305 x 2, 88311

c. 88300 x 2, 88311-51

d. 88300, 88305 x 2, 88311-51

56. Dr. Garcia, a pathologist, was consulted during surgery on Mr. Barber. Dr. Garcia was provided with two tissue blocks and five frozen sections from Mr. Barber's gallbladder. Additional cytologic examination by squash prep was required on two separate sites of the gallbladder specimens (one squash prep completed on tissue without

frozen section, one squash prep completed on tissue with frozen section). How should Dr. Garcia's professional services be reported?

a. 88329, 88332-26, 88334-26

b. 88304-26

c. 88331-26, 88334-26

d. 88331-26, 88332-26, 88333-26, 88334-26

57. What type of microorganism testing is identified in the CPT Professional Edition as: Colony morphology, growth on selective media, Gram stains or up to three tests (eg., catalase, oxidase, indole, urease)?

a. Presumptive

b. Definitive

c. Molecular

d. Compatibility

58. Sarah is being tested as a possible bone marrow donor for her brother. The laboratory completing the tests for HLA cross match used flow cytometry on two serum samples Sarah provided. How should you report these laboratory services?

a. 86835, 86826

b. 86829

c. 86825, 86826

d. 86831

Medicine

59. Which of the following must be included to report from code range 93040-93042?

a. A specific order for an electrocardiogram or rhythm strip followed by a separate, signed, written, and retrievable report

b. A verbal request for a consult including only a record review

c. A specific order for an electrocardiogram or rhythm strip followed by a separate, signed, verbal, and nonretrievable report

d. A written request for a consult including only a record review.

60. Cassidy, a 35-year-old patient, has a history of diabetes mellitus controlled with insulin. She was diagnosed with background diabetic retinopathy three years ago. Today, Cassidy was referred to Dr. Nelson for retinal images with fundus photography of both eyes. Upon completion of the images, Dr. Nelson reviewed the study and sent a detailed report back to the referring physician outlining the progression in Cassidy's condition. How should Dr. Nelson report, her services?

a. 99242-25, 92228, 92250-59   b. 92228

c. 99242-25, 92227, 92250-59   d. 92227

61. George, a 26-year-old patient, returned to Dr. Morris's office for his scheduled psychotherapy visit. In addition to the 45-minute psychotherapy session, Dr. Morris documented George's increased anxiety and depression, completed an expanded problem-focused history, expanded problem-focused examination, and documented low-complexity medical decision-making. Total time spent face-to-face with the patient was documented as 65 minutes. How should Dr. Morris report services for today's visit?

a. 99213, 90836

b. 99213, 90834

c. 99214, 90838

d. 99214, 90836

62. Brandi, a 14-year-old patient, underwent four daily end-stage renal dialysis services in the outpatient clinic prior to being hospitalized. A complete assessment was not provided before Brandi's hospitalization. How should you report the daily services?

a. 90957, 90969

b. 90965

c. 90957

d. 90969 x 4

63. Harper, a 55-year-old female patient is being tested for focal weakness and twitching of her lower extremity motor nerves. Today, she underwent three nerve conduction studies and a needle electromyography testing of three muscles. How should you report these services?

a. 95860, 95885

b. 95863, 95886

c. 95908, 95885

d. 95908, 95887

64. Dr. Risser treated a 44-year-old established patient with a history of CHF in the ER for acute shortness of breath and chest pain. After testing, Dr. Risser took the patient to the cardiac procedure suite with a diagnosis of an impending infarction. Dr. Risser completed a primary diagnostic PTCA to the left circumflex and left anterior descending artery. Following the PTCA, Dr. Risser determined that placement of three stents in the left anterior descending artery was indicated. He proceeded with placement of the stents during this same surgical session. How should Dr. Risser report his services for this procedure?

a. 99284-25, 92920, 92928 x 3

b. 92928, 92929 x 2

c. 92920, 92928-59, 92929-59

d. 92928, 92921

Anatomy

65. Cushing's syndrome may be caused by prednisone therapy. This syndrome is considered a disorder of what gland(s)?

a. Thymus

b. Testes

c. Ovarian

d. Adrenal

66. Which of the following describes the location of the femur?

a. Distal to the acetabulum and proximal to the patella

b. Proximal to the acetabulum and distal to the patella

c. Distal to the patella and proximal to the ischium

d. Proximal to the ischium and distal patella

67. Which of the following terms best reflects the function of the growth plate?

a. Longitudinal growth

b. Blood cell formation

c. Formation of synovial fluid

d. Apoptosis fragmentation

68. What bones make up the axial skeleton?

a. Spine, collar bone, arms

b. Skull, rib cage, spine

c. Shoulder bones, pelvic bones, arms and legs

d. Coccyx, ulna, femur, tibia

Terminology

69. What type of condition describes a patient diagnosed with oligospermia?

a. Knots in the varicose vein

b. Inflammation of the prostate gland

c. Abnormally low number of sperms in the semen

d. Failure to ovulate

70. Blepharoplasty describes what type of procedure?

a. Surgical reduction of the eyelids to remove excess fat, skin and muscle

b. Treatment for spider veins with injections of sclerotic solutions

c. Replacement of damaged skin with healthy tissue taken from the donor

d. Destruction of tissue by burning or freezing

71. Which term describes the death of a tissue resulting from interrupted blood flow to that area?

a. Hypercirculation   b. Agglutination

c. Stenosis   d. Infarction

72. A patient's complaint for painful menstrual bleeding will be documented in the medical record as which of the following?

a. Amenorrhea   b. Dysmenorrhea

c. Menorrhagia   d. Metrorrhagia

Icd-10 Cm

73. Signs and symptoms that are associated routinely with a disease process should not be assigned as additional codes, unless otherwise instructed by classification.

a. True   b. False

74. Henry was playing baseball at the town's sports field and slid for home base where he collided with another player. He presents to the emergency department complaining of pain in the distal portion of his right middle finger. It is swollen and deformed. The physician orders an x-ray and diagnoses Henry with a displaced tuft fracture. He splints the finger, provides narcotics for pain, and instructs Henry to follow-up with his orthopedic in two weeks.

a. S62.632A, Y93.64, W51.XXXA, Y92.320

b. S62.662A, Y93.64, W03.XXXA, Y92.320   c. S62.392A, Y93.64, W51.XXXA, Y92.320   d. 562.632A, Y93.67, W03.XXXA, Y92.320

75. A newborn has been placed in NICU to treat herpetic vesicles on her torso and lower extremities. Tests have been ordered to rule out herpetic encephalitis, chorioretinitis and sepsis, and prophylactic protocols will be put in place to prevent spread of the infection from rupturing lesions. Code the patient's diagnosis.

a. B00.9

b. P35.2

c. P37.8

d. B00.0

76. Which of the following Z codes can be reported as a first listed code?

a. Z37.0

b. Z89.621

c. Z87.710

d. Z00.129

77. A 36-year-old who is pregnant in her 38th week with her first child is admitted to the hospital. She experiences a prolonged labor during the first stage and eventually births a healthy baby boy.

a. O63.0, O09.519, Z37.0

b. O80, Z37.0

c. O80, O63.0, O09.519, Z37.0

d. O63.0, O09.513, Z37.0

Hcpcs

78. During an emergency room visit, Sally was diagnosed with pneumonia. She was admitted to the hospital observation unit and treated with 500 mg of Zithromax through an IV route. How would you report the supply of this drug?

a. J0456

b. Q0144

c. J1190x2

d. J2020x2

79. Joe lost his ability to speak as a result of an accident. Today, he received a speech-generating synthesized device, which is activated by physical contact with the device. Which code would you report for supply of this device?

a. E2502

b. E2510

c. E2500

d. E2508

80. A patient has a home health aide come to his home to clean and dress a burn on his lower leg. The aide used a special absorptive sterile dressing to cover a 20 sq. cm. area. She also covers a 15 sq. cm. area with a self adhesive sterile gauze pad.

a. A6204, A6403

b. A6252, A6403

c. A6252, A6219

d. A6204, A6219

Compliance And Regulatory

81. What organization is responsible for updating CPT codes each year?

a. American Health Information Management Association (AHIMA)

b. American Academy of Professional Coders (AAPC)

c. American Medical Association (AMA)

d. Centre for Medicare and Medicaid Services (CMS)

82. Which of the following statements regarding advanced benefi-

ciary notices (ABN) is TRUE?

a. ABN must specify only the CPT® code that Medicare is expected to deny.

b. Generic ABN which states that a Medicare denial of payment is possible or the internist is unaware whether Medicare will deny payment or not is acceptable.

c. An ABN must be completed before delivery of items or services are provided.

d. An ABN must be obtained from a patient even in a medical emergency when the services to be provided are not covered.

83. Which of the following is an example of fraud?

a. Reporting the code for ultrasound guidance when used to perform a liver biopsy.

b. Reporting a biopsy and excision performed on the same skin lesion during the same encounter.

c. Failing to append modifier 26 on an X-ray that is performed in the physician's office.

d. Failure to append modifier 57 on the EM service performed the day prior to a minor procedure.

Coding Guidelines

84. What is the time limit for reporting diagnosis codes for late effects?
    a. Three months   b. Six months
    c. One year   d. No limit

85. Which of the following statements regarding the ICD-10-CM coding conventions is TRUE?

a. If the same condition is described as both acute and chronic and separate subentries exist in the Alphabetic Index at the same indentation level, code only the acute condition.

b. Only assign a combination code when the Alphabetic Index explanation directs the coder to use it.

c. An ICD-10-CM code is still valid even if it has not been coded to the full number of digits required for that code.

d. Signs and symptoms that are integral to the disease process should not be assigned as additional codes, unless otherwise instructed.

86. When using the CPT index to locate procedures, which of the following are considered primary classes for main entries?

a. Procedure or service; organ or other anatomic site; condition; synonyms, eponyms, and abbreviations

b. Abbreviations; signs and symptoms, anatomic site; and code assignment

c. Conventions; code ranges; modifying terms

d. Procedure or service; modifiers; clinical examples; and definitions

87. Which of the following code and modifier combinations are correct?

a. 0165T-25

b. 15003-51

c. 93572-51

d. None of the above

88. In which position should you sequence a manifestation code in brackets [ ]?

a. Primary code

b. Primary code in newborn cases

c. Secondary code to an underlying condition

d. Parenthesis

89. Which types of contrast administration alone do not qualify as a study "with contrast'?

a. Oral and/or extravascular intrathecal

b. Oral and/or

c. Oral and/or intravascular or rectal

d. Oral and/

90. Which of the following place of service codes is reported for fracture care performed by an orthopedic physician in the urgent care facility?

a. 11

b. 20

c. 22

d. 23

Coding Case Studies

91. What codes should you report for Dr. West in this case?

Preoperative Diagnosis: Right knee medial meniscal tear.

Postoperative Diagnosis: Current, right knee medial meniscal tear with mild grade three chondral change in the medial femoral condyle.

Procedure: Right knee arthroscopy with medial meniscectomy.

Summary of procedures: A 52-year-old male patient signed

consent forms and was taken to the surgical suite. After adequate anesthesia was obtained, a tourniquet was applied to the right thigh. Examination of the right knee under anesthesia showed full range of motion. No instability to provocative testing. The left lower extremity was placed in a well leg holder. The right lower extremity was then prepped and draped in usual sterile fashion.

Anteromedial and anterolateral portals were established after distention of soft tissues with 20 cc of 0.5% Marcaine with epinephrine. The arthroscope was inserted with a blunt trocar and the joint distended with lactated Ringer's. Examination of the medial compartment showed a tear in the posterior root of the medial meniscus right at the intersection which was unstable to probing. This area was debrided with punch, motorized shaver, and electrocautery unit until stable. There was a mild grade-three change on the medial lateral compartment that showed normal articular cartilage and a stable lateral meniscus to probing. The anterior compartment showed normal articular cartilage and no loose bodies. The joint was copiously irrigated with lactated Ringer's and the instruments were removed. The wounds were closed with 4-0 nylon suture in an interrupted fashion. The joint was injected with additional 10 cc of 0.5% Marcaine with epinephrine and 2 mg of estradiol. Sterile dressings were applied. The patient was awakened and brought to recovery room in stable condition. The tourniquet was applied but not inflated and blood loss was minimal. The patient tolerated the procedure well.

a. M23.205, 29880-RT

b. M23.205, 29881-RT

c. S83.232A, 29881-RT

d. S83.232A, 29880-RT

92. What codes should Dr. Field report for his service in the following case? Preoperative Diagnosis: Adenotonsillar hypertrophy and obstructive sleep apnea.

Postoperative Diagnosis: Same.
Procedure: Tonsillectomy and Adenoidectomy
Anesthesia: General by endotracheal tube by Dr. Rush

Operative report: The patient is a 10-year-old female with a history of adenotonsillar hypertrophy as well as symptoms of sleep apnea. Informed consent was obtained from parents and the risks of surgery explained. The patient was taken to the operating room and placed in the supine position. Shoulder roll was placed. McIvor mouth retractor was used to retract the tongue inferiorly. Red rubber catheter was used to retract the palate superiorly. Adenoids were inspected and found to be enlarged and obstructed in the nasopharynx. They were removed with an adenoid curette. The area was then packed with tonsil sponges soaked in Marcaine. The right tonsil and then the left tonsil were grasped with curved Allis and removed with Bovie cautery. The regions were then further cauterized with suction cautery and 4 cc of 0.25% Marcaine was injected in the field. The patient tolerated the procedure well, and blood loss was minimal; patient was awakened and taken to recovery room in stable condition.

a. J35.1, J35.2, 42820	b. J35.3, 42821

c. J35.1, J35.2, 42820	d. J35.3, 42820

93. What codes should Dr. Stone report in the following case?

Brief history of present illness: 26-year-old female with a history of nephrolithiasis. She complains of left-sided flank discomfort with hematuria, dysuria, and passage of fragments. This morning she presented to ER with increased left and right side flank pain. She underwent CT with contrast of the abdomen and pelvis showing approximately 8 right renal calculi ranging between 2 and 12 mm and 10 left renal calculi ranging between 5 and 8 mm with possible nephrocalcinosis based on the radiologist's interpretation. Dr. Stone, the urologist, consulted with patient, reviewed results of the CT scan, and discussed treatment options. The patient signed an informed consent for the following procedure.

Postoperative diagnosis: Bilateral nephrolithiasis

Procedure: Lithotripsy, extracorporeal shock wave. She was given 1 g Ancef, brought to the operating room, placed supine on the lithotropsy table. Using fluoroscopy, the right and left kidneys were evaluated with no overlying bowel gas, stool, or bowel contents; multiple stones were visualized (R. 8 and L. 10). The ureters were examined showing no stones or fragments present. Stones were targeted for treatment via extracorporeal shock wave with successful break down and flush. After treatment the patient was awoken in the operating room and extubated without difficulty. She was taken to recover in stable condition.

a. N20.1, N20.0, 50590

b. N20.0, 74177, 50590

c. N20.0, N20.1, R10.30, 50590

d. N20.0, 50590

94. What codes should Dr. Orange report in the following case?

Surgeon: Dr. Orange Anesthesiologist: Dr. Mee

Preoperative Diagnosis: Prominent left spermatocele Postoperative Diagnosis: Same

Procedure performed: Left spermatocystectomy with epididymectomy

Indications for procedure: The patient is a 66-year-old male with a progressively enlarging left-sided spermatocele causing discomfort in this area. This lesion is 4 times the size of the testicle. After careful explanation of the risks, benefits, and alternatives, he agreed to the procedure.

Operative report: The patient was taken to the operating room, prepped and draped in the usual fashion, and induced under general anesthesia. He was placed in a supine position. Midline raphe incision was made using a skin knife, Bovie electrocautery was used to dissect through the subcutaneous tissues down to the level of the tunica vaginalis, which was incised. The testicle and spermatocele were exposed. A portion of the epididymis was overlying the spermatocele and I dissected this carefully with resection of a portion of the epididymis, which was tied off using a 3-0 Vicryl free tie. I proceeded to dissect circumferentially to free the spermatocele leaving adequate blood supply to the testicle. The testicle was placed back within the tunica vaginalis; proceeded to reapproximate this without difficulty using a 3-0 Vicryl stitch. Subcutaneous closure was performed using a 3-0 Vicryl in a running fashion, followed by closure of the skin using 3-0 chromic in a running horizontal mattress fashion. The patient tolerated the procedure well with no complications. He was taken to the recovery room in satisfactory condition.

a. Q52.8, 54860-LT, 54840-LT

b. Q52.8, 54840-LT

c. N43.40, 54860-LT

d. N43.40, 54840-LT

95. What codes should Dr. Rogers report in the following case?

Preoperative Diagnosis: Cervical stenosis with left upper extremity radiculopathy Postoperative Diagnosis: Same

Procedure: Cervical epidural steroid injection at C4-C5 directed to the left midline with fluoroscopic guidance.

Anesthesia: Local

Indications: Fluoroscopy is utilized to confirm placement of the needle within the epidural spaces and rule out any vascular uptake. Epidural steroid injections performed to reduce swelling and inflammation as an adjunct to rehabilitation of the spine.

Procedure: Dr. Rogers explained the procedure and risks and benefits to her 42-year- old male patient. The patient agreed to the procedure and signed consent forms. The patient was escorted to the procedure suite and laid in a prone position on the procedure table. The skin of the cervicothoracic region was scrubbed and draped in the usual sterile fashion. C4-C5 interspace was identified. Overlying skin was anesthetized with 1% buffered lidocaine. An 18-guage 3 1/2-inch Tuohy epidural needle was slowly
advanced through the aforementioned interspace until the ligamentum flavum was perforated with a loss-of-resistance technique. Aspiration was negative for CSF or blood, and contrast was slowly infiltrated, demonstrating appropriate epidural spread on PA and lateral views without vascular uptake or intrathecal flow in either view. Final aspiration was likewise negative and 9 mg of Betamethasone was slowly infiltrated through the needle. The needle was then removed. The patient tolerated the procedure well and was transported to the recovery room for postprocedural observation. He experienced no complications and was discharged in stable and satisfactory condition in the company of a driver. He will follow up in

the office in two weeks and by phone for any questions in the interim.

a. M48.02, M54.12, 62320, 77003-26

b. M48.02, M54.12, 62320

c. M50.00, M48.02, M54.12, 62324, 77003-26

d. M54.2, M48.02, 62320, 62322

96. Preoperative diagnosis: Left knee medial collateral ligament tear. Anterior cruciate ligament tear. Possible meniscus tear

Postoperative diagnosis: Same

Proceures:

Left knee medial collateral liga mentear:

Exam under anesthesia Anterior cruciate

ligament tear: Diagnostic arthroscopy of

left knee Possible meniscus tear: Left knee

arthroscopic repair of lateral meniscus

Tourniquet time: 2.5 hours

Procedure: The patient was taken to the operating room and positioned, and an epidural anesthetic was placed. Once the anesthetic had taken effect, the patient's left leg was examined under anesthesia and noted to have increased valgus laxity with end point, a positive Lachman test, and positive pivot-shift test. The patient was prepped and draped in the normal fashion, exsanguinated, and the tourniquet applied to a 350 mmHg. The knee was then insufflated and irrigated with fluid. Using the arthroscopic sheath, visualization of the knee joint began. Attention was turned to the lateral meniscus where the tear was debrided. Using the arthroscope, the lateral meniscus was sutured with two mattress-type sutures of non-absorbable 2-0 material. The sutures were then tied and visualized with arthroscopy to reveal the meniscus to be in excellent shape and stable position. The 3.5-cm wound was thoroughly irrigated and closed with intermediate subcutaneous sutures. A sterile compression dressing was applied. The patient was placed in a TED hose and Watco brace, setting the brace between 40º and 60º of free motion. He was then taken to the recovery room in stable condition. The instrument, sponge, and needle counts were correct.

a. 29882, 29877-52, 29870-51

b. 29866, 29868

c. 29870, 29882, 12032

d. 29882

97. Dr. Manning, a thoracic surgeon, was asked to consult with Nancy, a 66-year-old female with atherosclerotic heart disease. The patient, who requested the visit, is well known to Dr. Manning, who performed thoracic surgery on her two years ago. She was seen in his office Monday morning for a consultative visit with mild complaints of fatigue and shortness of breath. Dr. Manning dictated comprehensive history, comprehensive examination, and high-complexity decision-making. During this consultation, Dr. Manning made the decision to re operate on Nancy. He sent a written report back to her cardiologist, Dr. Shaw, regarding the need for another surgery to take place the following day. Monday evening, Nancy was admitted to the hospital to start the prep for the planned bypass surgery Tuesday morning.

Tuesday's operative report

Preoperative diagnosis: Atherosclerotic

heart disease Postoperative diagnosis:

Same

Anesthesia: General

Procedure: The patient was brought to the operating room and placed in the supine position. With the patient under general intubation anesthesia, the anterior chest, abdomen, and legs were prepped and draped in the usual fashion. Review of a postoperative angiography showed severe, recurrent, two-vessel disease with normal ventricular function. A segment of the femoropopliteal artery was harvested using endoscopic vein-harvesting technique and prepared for grafting. The patient was heparinized and placed on cardiopulmonary bypass. The patient was cooled as necessary for the remainder of the procedure and an aortic cross-clamp was placed. The harvested vein was anastomosed to the aorta and brought down to the circumflex and anastomosed into place. An artery was anastomosed to the left subclavian artery and brought down to the left anterior descending and anastomosed into place. The aortic cross-clamp was removed after 55 minutes with spontaneous cardio version to a normal sinus rhythm. The patient was warmed and weaned from the bypass without difficulties after 104 minutes. The patient achieved homeostasis. The chest was drained and closed in layers in the usual fashion. The leg was closed in the usual fashion. Sterile dressings were applied and the patient returned to intensive care recovery in satisfactory condition.

How should Dr. Manning report his services for

Monday and Tuesday in this case? a. Monday: 99255-57; Tuesday: 33511, 33517, 35600

b. Monday: 99215-57; Tuesday: 33533, 33517-51, 35572-80, 33530-51

c. Monday: 99255-57; Tuesday: 33533, 33510, 33572, 33530

d. Monday: 99215-57; Tuesday: 33533, 33517, 35572, 33530

98. How would the following case be coded?

Preoperative diagnosis: Lesion, buccal submucosa, right lower lip

Postoperative diagnosis: Same

Procedure performed: Excision of lesion, buccal submucosa, and right lower lip Anesthesia:

Local

Procedure: The patient was placed in the supine position. A measured 7x8 mm hard lesion is felt under the submucosa of the right lower lip. After application of 1% Xylocaine with 1:1000 epinephrine, the lesion was completely excised. The lesion does not extend into the muscle layer. The 8-cm wound was closed with complex mattress sutures to the submucosal level and dressed in typical sterile fashion. The patient tolerated the procedure well and returned to the recovery area in satisfactory condition.

a. 40816, D10.39

b. 40814, 40831-51, D10.39

c. 40814, K13.79

d. 40814, D10.39

99. What codes should be reported with the following case? Preopera-

tive Diagnosis: Total retinal detachment, right eye Postoperative Diagnosis: Same

Procedure performed: Complex repair of retinal detachment with photocoagulation, scleral buckle, sclerotomy/vitrectomy

Anesthesia: Local

Procedure: The patient was placed, prepped, and draped in the usual manner. Adequate local anesthesia was administered. The operating microscope was used to visualize the retina, which has fallen into the posterior cavity. The vitreous was extracted using a VISC to complete the posterior sclerotomy. Minimal scar tissue was removed to release tension from the choroid. The retina was repositioned and attached using photocoagulation laser, a gas bubble, and a suture placement of a scleral buckle around the eye. The positioning of the retina was checked during the procedure to ensure proper alignment. Antibiotic ointment was applied to the eye prior to placement of a pressure patch. The patient tolerated the procedure well and returned to the recovery suite in satisfactory condition.

a. 67113-RT, 67107-51, 67145-51, 66990-51

b. 67113-RT, 69990-RT

c. 67113-RT, 66990-RT

d. 67107-51, 67145-51, 66990-51

100. What codes would the physician report for the following case?

Preoperative Diagnosis: Displaced impacted Colles fracture, left distal radius and ulna. Postoperative Diagnosis:

Same

Operative procedure: Reduction with application of internal fixator, left wrist fracture

FINDINGS: The patient is a 46-year-old right-hand-dominant female who fell off stairs 4 to 5 days ago sustaining an impacted distal radius fracture with possible intraarticular component and an associated ulnar styloid fracture. Today in surgery, fracture was reduced anatomically and an external fixator was applied.

PROCEDURE: Under satisfactory general anesthesia, the fracture was manipulated and C-arm images were checked. The left upper extremity was prepped and draped in the usual sterile orthopedic fashion. Two small incisions were made over the second metacarpal and after removing soft tissues including tendinous structures out of the way, frame was next placed and the site for the proximal pins was chosen. Small incision was drawing was carried out and blunt-tipped pins were placed for the EBI external fixator. The subcutaneous tissues were carried out of the way. The pin guide was placed and 2 drilled and blunt-tipped pins placed. Fixator was assembled. C-arm images were checked. Fracture reduction appeared to be anatomic. Suturing was carried out where needed with Vicryl interrupted subcutaneous and 4-0 nylon interrupted sutures. Sterile dressings were applied. Vascular supply was noted to be satisfactory. Final frame tightening was carried out.

A. 25600-LT, 20692-51

B. 25605- LT, 20690-51

C. 25606-LT

D. 25607

Exam - 2

1. The Medicare program is made up of several parts. Which part is affected by the Centers for Medicare and Medicaid Services - hierarchal condition categories (CMS-HCC)?
    a. Part A
    b. Part B
    c. Part C
    d. Part D

2. Healthcare providers are responsible for developing___and policies and procedures regarding privacy in their practices.
    a. Patient hotlines
    b. Work around procedures
    c. Fees
    d. Notices of Privacy Practices

3. How many components should be included in an effective compliance plan?
    a. 3
    b. 4
    c. 7
    d. 9

4. According to the AAPC Code of Ethics, Member shall use only_and_means in all professional dealings.
    a. private and professional
    b. efficient and inexpensive
    c. legal and profitable
    d. **legal and ethical**

5. Which option below is NOT a covered entity under HIPAA?
    a. Medicare
    b. Medicaid
    c. BCBS
    d. Worker's' Compensation

6. Muscle is attached to bone by what method?
   a. Tendons, ligaments, and directly to bone
   b. Tendons and aponeurosis
   c. Tendons, aponeurosis and directly to bone
   d. Tendons, ligaments, aponeurosis, and directly to bone

7. Which respiratory structure is comprised of cartilage and ligaments?
   a. Alveoli   c. Bronchiole
   b. Lung   d. Trachea

8. Upon leaving the last portion of the small intestine, nutrients move through the large intestine in what order?
   a. Cecum, transverse colon, ascending colon, descending colon, sigmoid colon, rectum, anus
   b. Cecum, ascending colon, transverse colon, descending colon, sigmoid colon, rectum, anus
   c. Cecum, ascending colon, transverse colon, sigmoid colon, descending colon, rectum, anus
   d. Cecum, descending colon, transverse colon, ascending colon, sigmoid colon, rectum, anus

9. What are chemicals which relay amplify and modulate signals between a neuron and another cell?
   a. Neurotransmitters   c. Interneurons
   b. Hormones   d. Myelin

10. A surgeon performs an "escharotomy." This procedure is best described as:
    a. Removal of scar tissue resulting from burns or other injuries
    b. Removal of a basal cell carcinoma
    c. Debridement of a pressure ulcer
    d. Removal of a fingernail

11. A vesiculotomy is defined as:

a. Removal of an obstruction from the vas deferens
   b. Surgical cutting into the seminal vesicles
   c. Removal of one of the seminal vesicles
   d. Incision into the prostate

12. A form of milk produced the first few days after giving birth is:

a. Chorion	c.	Colostrum
b. Lactose	d.	Prolactin

13. The root for pertaining to uterus is:

a. Cyt/o	c.	Pancreat/o
b. Hyster/o	d.	Endocrin/o

14. What is the meaning of "provider" in the ICD-10-CM guidelines refers to?
   a. the hospital   c. insurance Company
   b. the physician   d. the patient

15. When can you use the code for HIV (B20)?
   a. The test result is inconclusive
   b. The test result is confirmed by the physician's diagnostic statement
   c. Known HIV without symptoms
   d. Suspected HIV

16. The instructions and conventions of the classification take precedence over
   c. Physicians
   d. Official Coding Guidelines
   e. CPT®
   f. Nothing, they are only used in the event of no other instruction.

17. What diagnosis code(s) should be reported for spastic cerebral palsy due to meningitis?
    a. G03.9, G80.1
    b. G80.1, G09
    c. G80.1, G03.9
    d. G09, G80.1

18. 32-year-old sees her obstetrician about a lump in the right breast. Her mother and aunt both have a history of breast cancer. What diagnosis code(s) should be reported?
    a. N63, Z85.3
    b. N63.10
    c. C50.919, Z80.3
    d. N63.10, Z80.3

19. A 50-year old female visits her physician with symptoms of insomnia and upset stomach. The physician suspects she is pre-menopausal. His diagnosis is impending menopause. What diagnosis code(s) should be reported?
    a. G47.00, K30
    b. N92.0
    c. Z78.0, G47.09, K30
    d. Z78.0

20. When the type of diabetes mellitus is not documented in the medical note, what is used as the default type?
    g. Type II
    h. Type I
    c. Can be Type I or II
    d. Secondary

21. A patient is coming in for follow-up of his essential hypertension and cardiomegaly. Both conditions are stable and he is told to continue with his medications. What ICD-10-CM code(s) should be reported?
    a. I11.9, I51.7
    b. I51.7, I10
    c. I11.9
    d. I51.7

22. A 2-month-old is seeing his pediatrician for a routine health check examination. The physician notices a diaper rash and prescribes an ointment to treat it. What ICD-10-CM code(s) should be reported?
    a. L22
    b. Z00.121, L22
    c. L22, Z00.121
    d. Z00.129, L22

23. A patient is coming in for follow-up of a second-degree burn on the arm. The physician notes the burn is healing well. He is to come back in two weeks for another check-up. What ICD-10-CM code(s) should be reported?
    a. Z51.89, T22.20XA
    b. T22.20XD
    c. Z09, T22.20XD
    d. Z09

24. 40-year-old woman, 25-weeks-pregnant with her second child, is seeing her obstetrician. She is worried about decreased fetal movement. During the examination the obstetrician detects bradycardia in the fetus. What ICD-10-CM code(s) should be reported?
    a. O09.12, O09.413
    b. P29.12, O09.413
    c. O09.413, O09.522
    d. O09.522, O76

25. HCPCS Level II includes code ranges which consist of what type of codes?
    a. Category II codes, temporary national codes, miscellaneous codes, permanent national codes.
    b. Dental codes, morphology codes, miscellaneous codes, temporary national codes, permanent national codes.
    c. Permanent national codes, dental codes, category II codes.
    d. Permanent national codes, miscellaneous codes, dental codes, and temporary national codes.

26. A patient is seen in the OR for an arthroscopy of the medial compartment of his left knee. What is the correct coding to report for the Anesthesia services?
    a. 01400
    b. 01402
    c. 29870-LT
    d. 29880-LT

27. What is the correct CPT® code for the wedge excision of a nail fold of an ingrown toenail?

a. 11720   c. 11765
b. 11750   d. 11760

28. What is the code for partial laparoscopic colectomy with anastamosis and coloproctostomy?
    a) 44208   c) 44145
    b) 44210   d) 44207

29. What is the correct CPT® code for strabismus reparative surgery performed on 2 horizontal muscles?
    a. 67311   c. 67314
    b. 67312   d. 67316

30. What is commonly known as a boil of the skin?
    a. Abscess   c. Lesion
    b. Furuncle   d. Impetigo

31. A patient presents with a recurrent seborrheic keratosis of the left cheek. The area was marked for a shave removal. The area was infiltrated with local anesthetic, prepped and draped in a sterile fashion. The lesion measuring 1.8 cm was shaved using an 11-blade. Meticulous hemostasis was achieved using light pressure. The specimen was sent for permanent pathology. The patient tolerated the procedure well. What CPT® code(s) is reported?
    a. 11200   b. 11312
    c. 11442   d. 11642

32. A 45-year-old male with a previous biopsy positive for malignant melanoma, presents for definitive excision of the lesion. After induction of general anesthesia the patient is placed supine on the OR table, the left thigh prepped and draped in the usual sterile fashion. IV antibiotics are given, patient had previous MRSA infection. The previous excisional biopsy site on the left knee measured approximately 4 cm and was widely elipsed with a 1.5 cm margin. The excision was taken down to the underlying patellar fascia. Hemostasis was achieved via electrocautery. The resulting defect was 11cm x 5cm. Wide advancement flaps were created inferiorly and su-

periorly using electrocautery. This allowed skin edges to come together without tension. The wound was closed using interrupted 2-0 monocryl and 2 retention sutures were placed using #1 Prolene. Skin was closed with a stapler. What CPT® code(s) is/are reported?

    a. 27328   c. 14301, 27328-51
    b. 14301   d. 15738, 11606-51

33. Operative Report

PREOPERATIVE DIAGNOSIS: Diabetic foot ulceration.

POSTOPERATIVE DIAGNOSIS: Diabetic foot ulceration.

OPERATION PERFORMED: Debridement and split thickness autografting of left foot

ANESTHESIA: General endotracheal.

INDICATIONS FOR PROCEDURE: This patient with multiple complications from Type II diabetes has developed ulcerations which were debrided and homografted last week. The homograft is taking quite nicely; the wounds appear to be fairly clean; he is ready for autografting.

DESCRIPTION OF PROCEDURE: After informed consent the patient is brought to the operating room and placed in the supine position on the operating table. Anesthetic monitoring was instituted, internal anesthesia was induced. The left lower extremity is prepped and draped in a sterile fashion. Staples were removed and the homograft was debrided from the surface of the wounds. One wound appeared to have healed; the remaining two appeared to be relatively clean. We debrided this sharply with good bleeding in all areas. Hemostasis was achieved with pressure, Bovie cautery, and warm saline soaked sponges. With good hemostasis a donor site was then obtained

on the left anterior thigh, measuring less than 100 cm^2. The wounds were then grafted with a split-thickness autograft that was harvested with a patch of Brown dermatome set at 12,000 of an inch thick. This was meshed 1.5:1. The donor site was infiltrated with bupivacaine and dressed. The skin graft was then applied over the wound, measured approximately 60 cm² in dimension on the left foot. This was secured into place with skin staples and was then dressed with Acticoat 18's, Kerlix incorporating a catheter, and gel pad. The patient tolerated the procedure well. The right foot was redressed with skin lubricant sterile gauze and Ace wrap.

Anesthesia was reversed. The patient was brought back to the ICU in satisfactory condition. What CPT® and ICD-9-CM codes are reported?
    a. 15220-58, 15004-58, E10.621,L97.508
    b. 15120-58, 15004-58, E11.621, L97.529
    c. 15950-78, 15004-78, E11.622 ,L97.526
    d. 11044-78, 15120-78, E11.622 , L97.809

34. A patient is seen in the same day surgery unit for an arthroscopy to remove some loose bodies in the shoulder area. What CPT® code(s) should be reported?
    a. 29805   c. 29807
    b. 29806   d. 29819

35. A patient presented with a closed, displaced supracondylar fracture of the left elbow. After conscious sedation, the left upper extremity was draped and closed reduction was performed, achieving anatomical reduction of the fracture. The elbow was then prepped and with the use of fluoroscopic guidance, two K-wires were directed crossing the fracture site and pierced the medial cortex of the left distal humerus. Stable reduction was obtained, with full flexion and extension. K-wires were bent and cut at a 90 degree angle. Telfa padding and splint were applied. What CPT® code(s) should be reported?
    a. 24535   c. 24582
    b. 24538   d. 24566

36. A 27-year-old triathelete is thrown from his bike on a steep downhill ride. He suffered a severely fractured vertebra at C5. An anterior approach is used to dissect out the bony fragments and strengthen the spine with titanium cages and arthrodesis. The surgeon places the

patient supine on the OR table and proceeds with an anterior corpectomy at C5 with discectomy above and below. Titanium cages are placed in the resulting defect and morselized allograft bone is placed in and around the cages. Anterior Synthes plates are placed across C2-C3 and C3-C5, and C5-C6. What CPT® code(s) should be reported?

 a. 22326, 22554-51, 22845, 22851, 20930
 b. 63081, 22554-51, 22846, 22851, 20930
 c. 63001, 22554-51, 22845, 20931
 d. 22326, 22548-51, 22846, 20931

37. This 45-year-old male presents to the operating room with a painful mass of the right upper arm. General anesthesia was induced. Soft tissue dissection was carried through the proximal aspect of the teres minor muscle. Upon further dissection a large mass was noted just distal of the IGHL (inferior glenohumeral ligament), which appeared to be benign in nature. With blunt dissection and electrocautery, the 4-cm mass was removed en bloc and sent to pathology. The wound was irrigated, and repair of the teres minor with subcutaneous tissue was closed with triple-0 Vicryl. Skin was closed with double-0 Prolene in a subcuticular fashion. What CPT® code(s) should be reported?

 a. 23076-RT c. 23075-RT
 b. 23066-RT d. 11406-RT

38. A 50-year-old male had surgery on his upper leg one day ago and presents with serous drainage from the wound. He was taken back to the operating room for evaluation of the hematoma. His wound was explored, and there was a hematoma at the base of the wound, which was very carefully evacuated. The wound was irrigated with antibacterial solution.
What CPT® and ICD-10-CM codes should be reported?

 a. 10140-79, M96.840 c. 10140-76, L76.01

b. 27603-78, M96.840   d. 27301-78, M96.840

39. A patient presents with a healed fracture of the left ankle. The patient was placed on the OR table in the supine position. After satisfactory induction of general anesthesia, the patient's left ankle was prepped and draped. A small incision about 1 cm long was made in the previous incision. The lower screws were removed. Another small incision was made just lateral about 1 cm long. The upper screws were removed from the plate. Both wounds were thoroughly irrigated with copious amounts of antibiotic containing saline. Skin was closed in a layered fashion and sterile dressing applied. What CPT® code(s) should be reported?
    a. 20680
    b. 20680, 20680-59
    c. 20670
    d. 20680, 20670-59

40. A 31-year-old secretary returns to the office with continued complaints of numbness involving three radial digits of the upper right extremity. Upon examination, she has a positive Tinel's test of the median nerve in the left wrist. Anti-inflammatory medication has not relieved her pain. Previous electrodiagnostic studies show sensory mononeuropathy. She has clinical findings consistent with carpal tunnel syndrome. She has failed physical therapy and presents for injection of the left carpal canal. The left carpal area is prepped sterilely. A 1.5 inch 25 or 22 gauge needle is inserted radial to the palmaris longus or ulnar to the carpi radialis tendon at an oblique angle of approximately 30 degrees. The needle is advanced a short distance about 1 or 2 cm observing for any complaints of paresthesias or pain in a median nerve distribution. The mixture of 1 cc of 1% lidocaine and 10 mg of Kenalog is injected slowly along the median nerve. The injection area is cleansed and a bandage is applied to the site. What CPT® code(s) should be reported?
    a. 20526, J3301
    b. 20551, J3302
    c. 20526, J3303
    d. 20550, J3302

41. What CPT® code should be reported for a frontal

sinusotomy, nonobliterative, with osteoplastic flap, brow incision?
   a. 31080   c. 31084
   b. 31087   d. 31086

42. A 14-year-old boy presents at the Emergency Department experiencing an uncontrolled epistaxis. Through the nares, the ED physician packs his entire nose via anterior approach with medicated gauze. In approximately 15 minutes the nosebleed stops. What CPT® and ICD-10-CM codes should be reported?

   a. 30903-50, R04.0   c. 30901, R04.0
   b. 30901-50, R04.0   d. 30905, R04.0

43. A surgeon performs a high thoracotomy with resection of a single left lung segment on a 57-year-old heavy smoker who had presented with a six-month history of right shoulder pain. An apical lung biopsy had confirmed lung cancer. What CPT® and ICD-10-CM code(s) should be reported?
   a. 32100, C34.11, F17.219   c. 32503, C34.12, F17.210
   b. 32484, C34.12, F17.218   d. 19271, 32551-51, C34.10, M25.511, F17.218

44. Code the procedure for removal of two lobes of lungs, one from the right lung and other from the left lung with bronchoscopy.
   a. 32482   c. 32480-50
   b. 32484-50   d. 32482-50

45. Physician changes the old battery to a new battery on a patient's dual chamber permanent pacemaker.
   a. 33212   c. 33213, 33233-51
   b. 33229   d. 33228

46. A 35-year-old patient presented to the ASC for PTA of an obstructed hemodialysis AV graft in the venous anastomosis and the immediate venous outflow. The procedure was performed under moderate sedation admin-

istered by the physician performing the PTA. The physician performed all aspects of the procedure, including radiological supervision and interpretation & intraservice time is about 1 hour. Code for all services performed.
- a. 36903, 99151, 99153×3, 75989-26
- b. 36901, 99152, 99153×1, 75978-26
- c. 36902, 99152, 99153×3
- d. 35476, 99155, 99157×3, 75978-26

47. What is included in all vascular injection procedures?
    - a. Catheters, drugs, and contrast material
    - b. Selective catheterization
    - c. Just the procedure itself
    - d. Necessary local anesthesia, introduction of needles or catheters, injection of contrast media with or without automatic power injection, and/or necessary pre-and post injection care specifically related to the injection procedure.

48. **Preoperative Diagnosis**: Coronary artery disease associated with congestive heart failure; in addition, the patient has diabetes and massive obesity. Postoperative Diagnosis: Same Anesthesia: General endotracheal Incision: Median sternotomy

    Indications: The patient had presented with severe congestive heart failure associated with her severe diabetes. She had significant coronary artery disease, consisting of a chronically occluded right coronary artery but a very important large obtuse marginal artery coming off as the main circumflex system.
    She also has a left anterior descending artery, which has moderate disease and this supplies quite a bit of collateral to her right system. The decision was therefore made to perform a coronary artery bypass grafting procedure, particularly because she is so symptomatic. The patient was brought to the operating room.
    Description of Procedure: The patient was brought to the operating room and placed in supine position. Myself, the operating surgeon was scrubbed throughout the entire op-

eration. After the patient was prepared, median sternotomy incision was carried out and conduits were taken from the left arm as well as the right thigh. The patient weighs almost three hundred pounds and with her obesity there was some concern as to taking down the left internal mammary artery. Because the radial artery appeared to be a good conduit, she should have an arterial graft to the left anterior descending artery territory. She was cannulated after the aorta and atrium were exposed and after full heparinization. Attention was turned to the coronary arteries. The first obtuse marginal artery was a very large target and the vein graft to this target indeed produced an excellent amount of flow. Proximal anastomosis was then carried out to the foot of the aorta. The left anterior descending artery does not have severe disease but is also a very good target, and the radial artery was anastomosed to this target, and the proximal anastomosis was then carried out to the root of the aorta.

Sternal closure was then done using wires. The subcutaneous layers were closed using Vicryl suture. The skin was approximated using staples.

    a. 33533, 33510   c. 33533, 33517

    b. 33511   d. 33533, 33517, 35600

49. **CLINICAL SUMMARY**: The patient is a 55-year-old female with known coronary disease and previous left anterior descending and diagonal artery intervention, with recent recurrent chest pain. Cardiac catheterization demonstrated continued patency of the stented segment, but diffuses borderline changes in the ostial/proximal portion of the right coronary artery.

PROCEDURE: With informed consent obtained, the patient was prepped and draped in the usual sterile fashion. With the right groin area infiltrated with 2% Xylocaine and the patient given 2 mg of Versed and 50 mcg of fentanyl intravenously for conscious sedation and pain control, the 6-French catheter sheath from the diagnostic study was exchanged for a 6French sheath and a 6- French JR4 catheter with side holes utilized. The patient initially received 3000 units of IV heparin, and then IVUS interrogation was carried out using an Atlantis Boston Scientific probe. After it had been determined that there was significant stenosis in the ostial/

proximal segment of the right coronary artery, the patient received an additional 3000 units of IV heparin, as well as Integrilin per double-bolus injection. A 3.0, 16-mm-long Taxus stent was then deployed in the ostium and proximal segment of the right coronary artery in a primary stenting procedure with inflation pressure up to 12 atmospheres applied. Final angiographic documentation was carried out, and then the guiding catheter pulled, the sheath upgraded to a 7-French system, because of some diffuse oozing around the 6-French-sized sheath, and the patient is now being transferred to telemetry for post-coronary intervention observation and care. RESULTS: The initial guiding picture of the right coronary artery demonstrates the right coronary artery to be dominant in distribution, with luminal irregularities in its proximal and mid third with up to 50% stenosis in the ostial/proximal segment per angiographic criteria, although some additional increased radiolucency observed in that segment.

IVUS interrogation confirms severe, concentric plaque formation in this ostial/proximal portion of the right coronary artery with over 80% area stenosis demonstrated. The mid, distal lesions are not significant, with less than 40% stenosis per IVUS evaluation.

Following the coronary intervention with stent placement, there is marked increase in the ostial/proximal right coronary artery size, with no evidence for intimal disruption, no intraluminal filling defect, and TIMI III flow preserved.

CONCLUSION: Successful coronary intervention with drug-eluting Taxus stent placement to the ostial/proximal right coronary artery.

a. 92928-RC, 92978-RC   c. 92920-RC, 92978-51-RC
b. 92928-RC, 92924-RC, 92978-59RC
d. 92920-RC, 92924-59 RC, 92978-51-RC

50. What CPT® code(s) is/are reported for a percutaneous endoscopic direct placement of a tube gastrostomy for a patient who previously underwent a partial esophagectomy?
   a. 49440, 43116   c. 49440
   b. 43246, 43116   d. 43246

51. A patient suffering from cirrhosis of the liver presents with a history of coffee ground emesis. The surgeon diagnoses the patient with esophageal varices. Two days later, in the hospital GI lab, the surgeon ligates the varices with bands via an UGI endoscopy. What CPT® and ICD-10-CM codes are reported?
    a. 43205, I85.10
    b. 43244, K74.60, I85.10
    c. 43227, K74.60, I85.11
    d. 43235, I85.11

52. A 45-year-old patient with liver cancer is scheduled for a liver transplant. The patient's brother is a perfect match and will be donating a portion of his liver for a graft. Segments II and III will be taken from the brother and then the backbench reconstruction of the graft will be performed, both a venous and arterial anastomosis. The orthotopic allotransplantation will then be performed on the patient. What CPT® code(s) is/are reported?

    a. 47140, 47146, 47147, 47135
    b. 47141, 47146, 47135
    c. 47140, 47147, 47146, 47136
    d. 47141, 47146, 47136

53. Circumcision with adjacent tissue transfer was performed. What CPT® code(s) is/are reported for this service?
    a. 14040
    b. 54161-22
    c. 54163
    d. 54161, 14040

54. The patient presents to the office for CMG (cystometrogram) procedure(s). Complex CMG cystometrogram with voiding pressure studies is done, intrabdominal voiding pressure studies, and complex uroflow are performed. What CPT® code(s) is/are reported for this service?
    a. 51726
    c. 51728, 51797, 51741

b. 51726, 51728, 51797
d. 51728-26, 51797-26, 51741-26

55. **Preoperative diagnosis**: Cytologic atypia and gross hematuria

Postoperative diagnosis: Cytologic atypia and gross hematuria

Procedure performed: Cystoscopy and random bladder biopsies and GreenLight laser ablation of the prostate. Description: Bladder biopsies were taken of the dome, posterior bladder wall and lateral side walls. Bugbee was used to fulgurate the biopsy sites to diminish bleeding. Cystoscope was replaced with the cystoscope designed for the GreenLight laser. We introduced this into the patient's urethra and performed GreenLight laser ablation of the prostate down to the level of verumontanum (a crest near the wall of the urethra).
There were some calcifications at the left apex of the prostate, causing damage to the laser but adequate vaporization was achieved. What CPT® code(s) is/are reported for this service?

a. 52648, 52204
b. 52647
c. 52649, 52224-59
d. 52648, 52224-59

56. What is a root word for vagina?

a. Uter/o
b. Colp/o
c. Hyster/o
d. Metri/o

57. The patient presents with a recurrent infection of the Bartholin's gland which has previously been treated with antibiotics and I&D. At this visit her gynecologist incises the cyst, draining the material in it and tacks the edges of the cyst open creating an open pouch to prevent recurrence. How is this procedure coded?

a. 56405
b. 56420
c. 56440
d. 56740

58. What CPT® code is used to report a complete unilateral removal of the vulva and deep subcutaneous tissues?

    a. 56630   c. 56625
    b. 56633   d. 56620

59. Vulvar cancer in situ can also be documented as:

    a. VIN I   c. Adenocarcinoma of the vulva
    b. VIN II   d. VIN III

60. Patient wishes permanent sterilization and elects laparoscopic tubal ligation with falope ring. What is/are the CPT® code(s) reported for this service?

    a. 58671   c. 58615
    b. 58600   d. 58670

61. A patient presents with cervical cancer, it has spread and metastasized throughout the pelvic area. She receives a total abdominal hysterectomy with bilateral salpingo oophorectomy, cystectomy and creation of an ileal conduit and partial colectomy. What is/are the CPT® code(s) reported for this service?

    a. 58150, 51590, 44140
    b. 58152, 44141
    c. 58150, 51590, 44140, 58720
    d. 58240

62. A pregnant patient presents with the baby in a breech presentation. During the delivery the doctor attempts to turn the baby while it is still in the uterus. The baby turns but then immediately resumes his previous position. Can this service be billed? If so, what is the code?

    a. No, since the doctor was unable to successfully turn the baby.

b. No, this procedure is included in the obstetrical global package
c. Yes, since the doctor did the work, even though the outcome was unsuccessful. Report this procedure with code 59412
d. **Yes**, only billing it with postpartum care 59515

63. What are the four lobes of the brain?
    a. Frontal, Parietal, Temporal, Occipital
    b. Sulci, Cerebellum, Pons, Medulla
    c. Frontal, Cerebral, Cerebellum, Pons
    d. Frontal, Cerebrum, Temporal, Occipital

64. A neurosurgeon excised a berry aneurism outside the duramatter which was in the branches of anterior cerebral artery. The procedure was performed through orbitocranial approach into anterior cranial fossa
    a. 61584
    b. 61584, 61600
    c. 61584, 61600-51
    d. 61592

65. The physician removes the thymus gland in a 27-year-old female with myasthenia gravis. Using a transcervical approach, the blood supply to the thymus is divided and the thymus is dissected free from the pericardium and the thymus is removed. What CPT® code(s) is reported for this procedure?
    a. 60520
    b. 60521
    c. 60522
    d. 60540

66. A patient is having a decompression of the nerve root involving two segments of the lumbar spine via transpedicular approach. What CPT® code(s) is/are reported?
    a. 63056
    c. 63030, 63035

b. 63056, 63057   d. 63030

67. A patient with a herniated cervical disc undergoes a cervical laminotomy with a partial facetectomy and excision of the herniated disc for cervical interspace C3-C4.

What CPT® and ICD-10-CM codes are reported?
    a. 63050, M50.20   c. 63020, 63035, M50.20
    b. 63020, M50.20   d. 63050, M50.20

68. A 37-year-old has multilevel lumbar degenerative disc disease and is coming in for an epidural injection. Localizing the skin over the area of L5-S1, the physician uses the transforaminal approach. The spinal needle is inserted, and the patient experienced paresthesias into her left lower extremities. The anesthetic drug is injected into the epidural space. What CPT® code(s) is/are reported for this procedure?
    a. 64483, 64484
    b. 64493
    c. 64493, 64494
    d. 64483

69. A patient receives a paravertebral facet joint injection at three levels on both sides of the lumbar spine using fluoroscopic guidance for lumbar pain. What CPT® and ICD-10- CM codes are reported?
    a. 64493, 64494 x 2, M54.89
    b. 64493-50, 64494-50, 64495-50, M54.5
    c. 64493, 64495 x 2, M54.5
    d. 64495-50, M54.5

70. A 47-year old female presents to the OR for a partial corpectomy to three thoracic vertebrae. One surgeon performs the transthoracic approach while another surgeon performs the three vertebral nerve root decompressions necessary. How both providers do involved code for their por-

tions of the surgery?

    a. 63087-52, 63088-52 x 2

    b. 63085-62, 63086-62 x 2

    c. 63087-80, 63088-80 x 2

    d. 63085, 63086-82 x 2

71. A patient had recently experienced muscle atrophy and noticed she did not have pain when she cut herself on a piece of glass. The provider decides to obtain a biopsy of the spinal cord under fluoroscopic guidance. The biopsy results come back as syringomyelia.

What CPT® and ICD-10-CM codes are reported?

    a. 62270, G95.0, R20.9

    b. 62270, G95.0

    c. 62269, G95.0, R20.9

    d. 62269, G95.0

72. A 26-year-old patient presents with headache, neck pain, and fever and is concerned he may have meningitis. The patient was placed in the sitting position and given 0.5 mg Ativan IV. His back was prepped and a 20-gauge needle punctured the spine between L4 and L5 with the return of clear fluid. The cerebral spinal fluid was reviewed and showed no sign of meningitis. What CPT® code(s) is reported?

    a. 62270   c. 62282

    b. 62272   d. 62268

73. Patient had an abscess in the external auditory canal, which was drained in the office. What CPT® code(s) should be reported?

    a. 69540   c. 69020

    b. 69105   d. 69000

74. What CPT® code(s) should be reported for removal of foreign body from the external auditory canal w/o general anesthesia?
    a. 69205   c. 69200
    b. 69220   d. 69210

75. A patient with a cyst-like mass on his left external auditory canal was visualized under the microscope and a microcup forceps was used to obtain a biopsy of tissue along the posterior superior canal wall. What CPT® code(s) should be reported?
    a. 69100-RT   c. 69140-RT
    b. 69105-LT   d. 69145-LT

76. Following labor and delivery, the mother developed acute kidney failure. What ICD-10- CM code(s) is reported?
    a. O26.90   c. O90.4
    b. P01.9   d. N19

77. A 42-year-old patient was undergoing anesthesia in an ASC and began having complications prior to the administration of anesthesia. The surgeon immediately discontinued the planned surgery. If the insurance company requires a reported modifier, what modifier is reported best describing the extenuating circumstances?
    a. 53   c. 73
    b. 23   d. 74

78. Code 00350, Anesthesia for procedures on the major vessels of the neck, has a base value of ten (10) units. The patient is a P3 status, which allows one (1) extra base unit. Anesthesia start time is reported as 11:02, and the surgery began at 11:14. The surgery finished at 12:34 and the patient was turned over to PACU at 12:47, which was reported as the ending anesthesia time. Using fifteen-minute time increments and a conversion factor of $100, what is the correct anesthesia charge?
    a. $1,500.00   c. $1,700.00

b. $1,600.00   d. $1,800.00

79. A CRNA is personally performing a case, with medical direction from an anesthesiologist. What modifier is appropriately reported for the CRNA services?

    a. QY   c. QK
    b. QZ   d. QS

80. A 40-year-old female in good physical health is having a laparoscopic tubal ligation. The anesthesiologist begins to prepare the patient for surgery at 0830. Surgery begins at 0900 and ends at 1000. The anesthesiologist releases the patient to recovery nurse at 1015. What is the total anesthesia time and anesthesia code?

    a. 1hr 30 minutes, 00840   c. 1 hr, 00840
    b. 1hr 45 minutes, 00851   d. 1 hr 15 minutes, 00851

81. Procedure: Body PET-CT Skull Base to Mid Thigh

History: A 65-year-old male Medicare patient with a history of rectal carcinoma presenting for restaging examination. Description: Following the IV administration of 15.51 mCi of F-18 deoxyglucose (FDG), multiplanar image acquisitions of the neck, chest, abdomen and pelvis to the level of mid thigh were obtained at one-hour post-radiopharmaceutical administration. (Nuclear Medicine Tumor imaging).What CPT® code(s) is/are reported?

    a. 78815
    b. 78815, 96365
    c. 78816, 96365
    d. 78815, 96374

82. 25 year old female in her last trimester of her pregnancy comes into her obstetrician's office for a fetal biophysical profile (BPP). An ultrasound is used to first monitor the
fetus' movements showing three movements of the legs

and arms (normal). There are two breathing movements lasting 30 seconds (normal). Non-stress test (NST) of 30 minutes showed the heartbeat at 120 beats per minute and increased with movement (normal or reactive). Arms and legs were flexed with fetus' head on it chest, opening and closing of a hand. Two pockets of amniotic fluid at 3cm were seen in the uterine cavity (normal). Biophysical profile scored 9 out of 10 points (normal or reassuring).

What CPT® code(s) is/are reported
   by the obstetrician? a. 76818

   c. 76815

b. 76819   d. 59025, 76818

83. 65-year-old female has a 2.5 cm by 2.0 cm non small cell lung cancer in her right upper lobe of her lung. The tumor is inoperable due to severe respiratory conditions. She will be receiving stereotactic body radiation therapy under image guidance. Beams arranged in 8 fields will deliver 25 Gy per fraction for 4 fractions. What CPT® and ICD- 10-CM codes are reported?

   a. 77435-26, C34.11, Z51.0

   b. 77371-26, C34.11

   c. 77373-26, Z51.0, C34.11

   d. 77431-26, Z51.0, C34.12

84. A patient with thickening of the synovial membrane undergoes a fluoroscopic guided radiopharmaceutical therapy joint injection on his right knee. What CPT® code(s) is/are reported by the physician if performed in an ASC setting?

   a. 79440   c. 79999, 77002

   b. 79440, 20610   d. 79440-26, 77002-26, 20610.

85. A patient with bilateral lower extremity deep venous thromboses has a history of a recent pulmonary embolus. Under ultrasound guidance an inferior vena cavagram was performed demonstrating the right and left renal arteries at the

level of L1. A tulip filter device was passed down the sheath, positioned, and deployed with excellent symmetry. It showed the filter between the renal veins and the confluence of the iliac veins but well above the bifurcation of the inferior vena cava. What CPT® code(s) is reported?

    a. 75825   c. 75820
    b. 75827   d. 75860

86. An oncology patient is having weekly radiation treatments with a total of seven conventional fractionated treatments broken up five on one day and two on the next.
What radiology code is appropriate for this series of clinical management fractions?
    a. 77427   c. 77427x2
    b. 77427x7   d. 77427-22

87. A patient in her 2nd trimester with a triplet pregnancy is seen for an obstetrical ultrasound only including fetal heartbeats and position of the fetuses. What CPT® code(s) is/are reported for the ultrasound?
    a. 76805, 76810, 76810   c. 76815 x 3
    b. 76811, 76812, 76812   d. 76815

88. In what section of the Pathology chapter of CPT® would a coder find codes for a FISH test?
    a. Cytopathology   c. Chemistry
    b. Immunology   d. Other Procedures

89. A patient has a severe traumatic fracture of the humerus. During the open reduction procedure, the surgeon removes several small pieces of bone embedded in the nearby tissue. They are sent to Pathology for examination without microscopic sections. The pathologist finds no evidence of disease. How should the pathologist code for his services?
    a. This service cannot be billed   c. 88300

b. 88304   d. 88309, 88311

90. A patient presents with right upper quadrant pain, nausea, and other symptoms of liver disease as well as complaints of decreased urination. Her physician orders an albumin; bilirubin, both total and direct; alkaline phosphatase; total protein; alanine amino transferase; aspartate amino transferase, and creatinine. What CPT® code(s) is/are reported?

    a. 82040, 82247, 82248, 84075, 84155, 84460, 84450, 82565
    b. 80076, 82565
    c. 80076
    d. 80076-22

91. A urine pregnancy test is performed by the office staff using the Hybritech ICON (qualitative visual color comparison test). What CPT® code(s) is reported?

    a. 84703   c. 81025
    b. 84702   d. 81025, 36415

92. A pediatrician is asked to be in the room during the delivery of a baby at risk for complications. The pediatrician is in the room for 45 minutes. The baby is born and is completely healthy, not requiring the services of the pediatrician. What CPT® code(s) does the pediatrician report?

    a. 99219   c. 99360
    b. 99252   d. 99360 x 2

93. An infant is born six weeks premature in rural Arizona and the pediatrician in attendance intubates the child and administers surfactant in the ET tube while waiting in the ER for the air ambulance. During the 45 minute wait, he continues to bag the critically ill patient on 100 percent oxygen while monitoring VS, ECG, pulse oximetry and temperature. The infant is in a warming unit and an umbilical vein line was placed for fluids and in case of emergent needs for medications. How is this coded?

    a. 9929
    b. 99471
    c. 99291, 31500, 36510, 94610
    d. 99434, 99464, 99465, 94610, 36510

94. Patient comes in today at four months of age for a checkup. She is growing and developing well. Her mother is concerned because she seems to cry a lot when lying down but when she is picked up she is fine. She is on breast milk but her mother has returned to work and is using a breast pump, but hasn't seemed to produce enough milk. **PHYSICAL EXAM**: Weight 12 lbs 11 oz, Height 25in., OFC 41.5 cm. HEENT: Eye: Red reflex normal. Right eardrum is minimally pink, left eardrum is normal. Nose: slight mucous Throat with slight thrush on the inside of the cheeks and on the tongue. LUNGS: clear. HEART: w/o murmur. ABDOMEN: soft. Hip exam normal. GENITALIA normal although her mother says there was a diaper rash earlier in the week.

    ASSESSMENT

Four month
old well check
Cold
Mild
thrush
Diaper
rash
PLAN:
Okay to advance to
baby foods Okay to
supplement with
Similac
Nystatin suspension for the thrush and creams for the diaper rash if it recurs
Mother will bring child back after the cold symptoms resolve for her DPT, HIB and polio What E/M code(s) are reported?

    a. 99212   c. 99391, 99212-25
        b. 99391   d. 99213

95. A new patient wants to quit smoking. The patient has constant cough due to smoking and some shortness of breath. No night sweats, weight loss, night fever, CP, headache, or dizziness. He has tried patches and nicotine gum, which has not helped. Patient has been smoking for 40 years and smokes 2 packs per day. He has a family history of emphysema. A limited three system exam was performed. Physician discussed the pros and cons of medications used to quit smoking in detail. Counseling and education done for 20 minutes of the 30 minute visit. Prescription for Chantrix and Tetracylcine were given. Patient to follow up in 1 month. We will consider chest X-ray and cardiac work up. Select the appropriate CPT code(s) for this visit:
   a. 99203
   b. 99204
   c. 99204, 99354
   d. 99214, 99354

96. A patient with coronary atherosclerosis underwent a PTCA in 2 vessels. What CPT® code(s) is/are reported?
   a. 92920, 92921
   b. 92920×2
   c. 92924
   d. 92925, 92996

97. Margaret has food allergies, comes to her physician for her weekly allergen immunotherapy that consists of two injections prepared and provided by the physician. What is the correct CPT code?
   a. 95125
   b. 95117
   c. 95131
   d. 95146

98. A baby was born with a ventricular septal defect (VSD). The physician performed a right heart catheterization and transcatheter closure with implant by percutaneous approach. What codes are reported?

a. 93530, 93581-59, Q21.9   c. 93530, Q24.0
b. 93581, Q21.0   d. 93530, 93591-59, Q21.0

99. 30-year-old male cut his left hand on a piece of aluminum repairing the gutter on his house. 6 days later, it became infected. He went to the intermediate care center in his neighborhood, his first visit there. The wound was very red and warm with purulent material present. The wound was irrigated extensively with sterile water and covered with a clean sterile dressing. An injection of Bicillin CR, 1,200,000 units was given. The patient was instructed to return in 3-4 days. The physician diagnosed open wound of the hand with cellulitis. A problem focused history and examination with a low MDM were performed.

What are the CPT and ICD-10-CM codes?

a. 96372, L02.113   c. 99203, 96372, J0558 x 12, L03.114
b. 99202, J0558 x 4, L03.119   d. 99284, L03.114

100. Mrs. Salas had 30 minutes of angin a decubitus and was admitted to the Coronary Care Unit with a diagnosis of R/O MI. The cardiologist (private practice based) takes her to the cardiac catheterization suite at the local hospital for a left heart catheterization. Injection procedures for selective coronary angiography and left ventriculography were performed and imaging supervision and interpretation for the selective coronary angiography and left ventriculography was provided. What CPT® code(s) are reported for the services?

a. 93452-26   c. 93453-26
b. 93458-26   d. 93453-26, 93462

Exam - 3

Surgery - Integumentry

1. James suffered a severe crushing injury to his left upper leg. Two days after surgery, Dr. Barnes completed a dressing change under general anesthesia. How would you report this service?

a. 16020-LT
b. 15852, 01232, J2060
c. 01232-P6
d. 15852-LT

2. Dr. Jess removed a 4.5 cm (excised diameter) cystic lesion from Amy's forehead. The ulcerated lesion was anesthetized with 20 mg of 1% Lidocaine and then elliptically excised. The wound was closed with a layered suture technique and a sterile dressing applied. The wound closure, according to Dr. Jess's documentation, was 5.3 cm. How would you report this procedure?

a. 11446, 12053-51
b. 11646, 12013-51
c. 11446, J2001 x 2, 12013-59
d. 11313, 12053-59

3. Martha has a non-healing wound on the tip of her nose. After an evaluation by Dr. Martino, a dermatologist, Martha is scheduled for a procedure the following week. Dr. Martino documented an autologous split thickness skin graft to the tip of Martha's nose. A simple debridement of granulated tissues is completed prior to the

placement. Using a dermatome, a split thickness skin graft was harvested from the left thigh. The graft is placed onto the nose defect and secured with sutures. The donor site is examined, which confirms good hemostasis. How would you report this procedure?

a. 99213-25, 15050
b. 15050, 15004, 15005-59
c. 15277, 11042-59
d. 15120

4. Dr. Alexis completed Moh's surgery on Ralph's left arm. She reported routine stains on all slides, mapping, and color coding of specimens. The procedure was accomplished in three stages with a total of seven blocks in the second stage. How would you report Dr. Alexis' services?

a. 17313, 17314-58, 17315-59, 88314-59
b. 17311, 17312 x 7
c. 17313, 17314 x 2, 17315 x 2
d. 17311, 88302, 17314 x 3, 17312 x 7

5. How should you code an excision of a lesion when completed with an adjacent tissue transfer or rearrangement?

a. The excision is always reported in addition to the adjacent tissue transfer or rearrangement.
b. The excision is not separately reported with adjacent tissue transfer or rearrangement codes.
c. Code only malignant lesions in addition to the adjacent tissue transfer or rearrangement codes.
d. Code the lesion with a modifier -51 and code in addition to the adjacent tissue transfer or rearrangement codes.

6. Tina fell from a step ladder while clearing drain gutters at her home. She suffered contusions and multiple lacerations. At the emergency room she received sutures

for lacerations to her arm, hand, and foot. The doctor completed the following repairs: superficial repair to the arm of 12.8 cm, a single-layered closure of 7.9 cm that required extensive cleaning and removal of glass from the hand, and a simple repair to the foot of 9.6 cm. How would you report the wound repairs?
a. 12034, 12036, 12046, 12007
b. 12034, 12006-51
c. 12044, 12006-51
d. 12005, 12004

Muskuloskeletal System

7. Sally suffered a burst fracture to her lumbar spine during a skiing accident. Dr. Phyllis performed a partial corpectomy to L2 by a transperitoneal approach followed by anterior arthrodesis of L1-L3. She also positioned anterior instrumentation and placed a structural allograft to L1-L3. How would Dr. Phyllis report this procedure?
a. 63090, 22558-51, 22585, 22845, 20931
b. 63085, 22533, 22585-51, 22808-59
c. 22612 x 2, 22808, 22840-51, 20931
d. 22585, 22585-51, 22845-51, 20931-59

8. A patient suffered a fracture of the femur head. He had an open treatment of the femoral head with a replacement using a medicon alloy femoral head and methyl methacrylate cement. How would you report this procedure?
a. 27236
b. 27235
c. 27238

d. 27275, 27236-59

9. A patient suffered a penetrating knife wound to his back. A surgeon performed wound exploration with enlargement of the site, debridement, and removal of gravel from the site. The surgeon decided a laparotomy procedure was not necessary at this time. How would you report this procedure?
a. This procedure is bundled with the laparotomy
b. 49000, 97602-51, 20100-59
c. 49000, 20102-59
d. 20102

10. While playing at home, Riley dislocated his patella, when he fell from a tree. The surgeon documented an open dislocation. Riley underwent a closed treatment under anesthesia. How would you report the treatment and diagnoses?
a. 27420, S83.006A
b. 27562, S83.006A, W14.XXXA, Y92.017
c. 27840, 27562-51, S83.006A, W14.XXXA
d. 27560, S83.006A

11. Sarah presented to her primary care physician with pain and swelling in the right elbow. After careful examination he referred her to an orthopedic surgeon for a second opinion. Dr. Femur diagnosed Sarah with acute osteomyelitis of the olecranon process and recommended surgery. Sarah agreed to the surgery and underwent a sequestrectomy, through a posterior incision, with a loose repair over drains ending the procedure. Dr. Femur sent a written report back to Sarah's primary care physician along with the operative report. How would you report the procedure?
a. 99244-57, 24138-RT

b. 99214, 99244-57
c. 24138-RT
d. 99214, 23172-59

12. How should you report a deep biopsy of soft tissue of the thigh and knee area? a. 27323   b. 27324   c. 20206   d. 27328

Respiratory & Cardiovascular System

13. Julie, a 28-year-old ESRD patient was seen by Dr. Jeri in an outpatient hospital facility for treatment of an obstructed hemodialysis AV graft. Dr. Jeri provided moderate conscious sedation to Julie for percutaneous transluminal balloon angioplasty of the venous portion of the graft. This procedure lasted 45 minutes. Julie had an excellent result and was released to home after recovery from the treatment. Dr. Jeri performed the professional radiological supervision and interpretation with this procedure. What code(s) capture this service?

a. 36902
b. 36902, 36907
c. 36818
d. 36901, 36902

14. What code would you report for a cervical approach of a mediastinotomy with exploration, drainage, removal of   foreign body, or biopsy?
a. 39010   b. 39000   c. 39200
d. 39401

15. Roger had a rhinoplasty to correct damage caused by a broken nose. One year later he had a secondary rhinoplasty with major revisions. At the end of the

second surgery the incisions were closed with a single layer technique. How would you report the second procedure?

a. 30450
b. 30450-78
c. 30420, 12014
d. 30430, 12014-59

16. A surgeon started with a diagnostic thoracoscopy. During the same surgical session she completed a surgical thoracoscopy to control a hemorrhage. How would you report this procedure?

a. 32601
b. 32601, 32654-59
c. 32110
d. 32654

17. Dr. Sacra performed a CABG surgery on Fred five months ago. Today, Dr. Sacra completed another coronary artery bypass using three venous grafts with harvesting of a femoropopliteal vein segment. How would Dr. Sacra report her work for the current surgery?

a. 33512, 33530-51, 35572-51
b. 33535, 35500-51, 33519
c. 33512, 33530, 35572
d. 33535, 33519, 33530-51, 35500

18. Mrs. Reyes had a temporary ventricular pacemaker placed at the start of a procedure. This temporary system was used as support during the procedure only. How would you report the temporary system?

a. 33210
b. 33211
c. 33207
d. 33210, 33207-51, 33235-51

Digestive System

19. A patient comes in for surgery today to address complications from his previous partial enterectomy performed 5 months ago. Upon reopening the pa-

tient's previous incision the surgeon resected the ileum and a portion of the colon. An ileocolostomy was performed to complete the procedure with no complications. The appropriate CPT code to report is:

a. 44144
b. 44160
c. 44150
d. 44205

20. Dr. Blue performs a secondary closure of the abdominal wall for evisceration (outside the postoperative period). He opens the former incision and removes the remaining sutures; necrotic fascia is debrided down to viable tissue. The abdominal wall is then closed with sutures. How would you report the closure?

a. 11043
b. This is a bundled procedure and not reported
c. 39541
d. 49900

21. Heather lost her teeth following a motorcycle accident. She underwent a posterior, bilateral vestibuloplasty, which allows her to wear complete dentures. How would you report this procedure?

a. 40845, 15002
b. 40843-50
c. 40844
d. 40843

22. Dr. Erin is treating a 58-year-old male patient with a history of chewing tobacco. Dr. Erin finds a 3.4 cm tumor at the base of his tongue. She places needles under fluoroscopic guidance for sub sequential interstitial radioelement application. How would you report the professional services?

a. 41019, 77002-26

b. 41019, 77012-26, 77021-26
c. 61770, 41019-59
d. 77002

23. An 88-year-old male patient suffering from dementia accidentally pulled out his gastrostomy tube during the night. Dr. Keys, an interventional radiologist, takes him into an angiography suite, administers moderate sedation (an independent observer was present during the procedure), probes the site with a catheter and injects contrast medium for assessment 6 and tube placement. Dr. Keys finds that the entry site remains open and replaced the tube into the proper position. The intra-service time for the procedure took 45 minutes. How would Dr. Keys report his services?

a. 49440, 99156, 99157 x 2
b. 49440, 49450-59
c. 49450, 99152, 99153 x 2
d. 49450

24. Katherine had a hernioplasty to repair a recurrent ventral incarcerated hernia with implantation of mesh for closure. The surgeon completed debridement for necrotizing soft tissue due to infection.
How would you report this procedure?

a. 49566, 11005-51, 49568
b. 49565, 11005-51, 49568
c. 49565
d. 49525, 11006, 49568-51

Genitourinary System

25. A patient had a renal auto-transplantation extracorporeal surgery, reimplantation of a kidney, and a

partial nephrectomy. How would you report this procedure?
a. 50340, 50380, 50240-51
b. 50543, 50370-52
c. 50380, 50240-51
d. 50380, 50240-59

26. Bill, a 52-year-old male patient, was admitted to the hospital and treated for prostatic malignancy. His doctor dictated a detailed history, detailed exam, and straightforward medical decision-making for admission. He was treated with interstitial transperineal prostate brachytherapy, including implantation of 51 iodine-125 seeds. His doctor visited him the day after the procedure. How would you report the professional service by the therapeutic radiologist who did both the implantation and brachytherapy?
a. 99222, 55876, 77763 x 51
b. 55875, 77778
c. 99221, 55875, 77785
d. 58346, 77799 x 125

27. Harry had a couple of stones in both kidneys. He was taken into the lithotripsy unit and placed on the lithotripsy table in a supine position with the induction of anesthesia. The stones were well visualized and the patient received a total of 3,500 shocks with a maximum power setting of 3.0. The treatment was successful. How would you report this procedure?
a. 50590
b. 50561
c. 50060
d. 50080

28. Alex suffered several injuries to his upper leg muscles and penis when he fell onto the bar of his

touring bicycle. The day of the accident, Dr. Green completed muscle repair surgery to Alex's upper legs. Today, three days after the leg surgeries, Dr. Green took Alex back to the operating suite to complete an unrelated repair to the penis. Dr. Green completed a plastic repair to correct the penal injury. What code(s) would capture today's procedure?

a. 54440-79
b. 27385, 54440-59
c. 27393, 54620-79
d. 54440-26

29. A 65-year-old male patient has an indwelling nephroureteral double-J stent tube replaced to treat a ureteral obstruction caused by a stricture from postoperative scarring. His stent tube is exchanged every two months to prevent occlusion in the stent, UTI, and loss of kidney function. Dr. Mott did this procedure via a transurethral approach under conscious sedation and provided the radiological supervision and interpretation. How would you report this procedure?

a. 50605, 50382
b. 50385, 52283, 99152
c. 50385
d. 53855

30. Dr. Blue provided interpretation and results for a needle electromyography for anal sphincter function. How would you report this service?

a. 51784
b. 51784, 51785-51
c. 55875
d. 51785-26

Nervous System, Eye & Ear

31. An infant born at 33 weeks underwent five photocoagulation treatments to both eyes due to ret-

inopathy of prematurity at six months of age. The physician used an operating microscope during these procedures. These treatments occurred once per day for a defined treatment period of five days. How would you report all of these services?

a. 67229 -50
b. 67229 x 5
c. 67229, 69990
d. 67229

32. Todd had a tumor removed from his left temporal bone. How would you report this service?
a. 61563   b. 61500
c. 69979, 69990-51   d. 69970

33. Jennifer was admitted to the hospital for an aspiration of two thyroid cysts. Her physician completed this procedure with CT guidance of the needle including interpretation and report. How would you report the professional services?

a. 60300-26, 76942-26
b. 60300 x 2, 77012-26
c. 10022, 60300-51, 77012-26
d. 60300

34. Baby Smith was diagnosed with meningitis. His physician placed a needle through the fontanel at the suture line to obtain a spinal fluid sample on Monday. The needle was withdrawn and the area bandaged. The baby required another subdural tap bilaterally on Wednesday. How would you report Wednesday's service?

a. 61001
b. 61000, 61001
c. 61070
d. 61001-50

35. After a snow skiing accident, Barry had a cervical laminoplasty to four vertebral segments. How should

you report this procedure?
a. 63050 x 4
b. 22600, 63051-51
c. 22842, 63045, 63050
d. 63050

36. How is a neuroplasty procedure described in the CPT Professional Edition?

a. The decompression or freeing of intact nerve from scar tissue, including external neurolysis and/or transposition.
b. The surgical repair of nerves using only microscopic techniques.
c. The position of nerves tested one or more anatomic digits.
d. The decompression or freeing of an intact vein from scar tissue, including external neurolysis and/or transposition.

Evaluation & Management

37. How does the CPT Professional Edition define a new patient?

a. A new patient is one who has not received any professional services from the physician or another physician of the same specialty who belongs to the same group practice, within the past two years.
b. A new patient is one who has not received any professional services from the physician or another physician of the same specialty who belongs to the same group practice, within the past three years.
c. A new patient is one who has received professional services from the physician or another physician of the same specialty within the last two years for the same problem.
d. A new patient is one who has received hospital services but has never been seen in the clinic by the reporting physician.

38. James, a 35-year-old new patient, received 45

minutes of counseling and risk factor reduction intervention services from Dr. Kelly. Dr. Kelly talked to James about how to avoid sports injuries. Currently, James does not have any symptoms or injuries and wants to maintain this status. This was the only service rendered. How would you report this service?

a. 99213
b. 99203
c. 99385
d. 99403

39. Andrea, a 52-year-old patient, had a hysterectomy on Monday morning. That afternoon, after returning to her hospital room, she suffered a cardiac arrest. A cardiologist responded to the call and delivered one hour and 35 minutes of critical care. During this time the cardiologist ordered a single view chest x-ray and provided ventilation management. How should you report the cardiologist's services?

a. 99291, 99292
b. 99291, 99292, 94002
c. 94002, 99231
d. 99291, 99292, 99292-52

40. Brandon was seen in Dr. Shaw's office after falling off his bunk bed. Brandon's mother reported that Brandon and his sister were jumping on the beds when she heard a "thud." Brandon complained of knee pain and had trouble walking. Dr. Shaw ordered a knee x-ray that was done at the imaging center across the street. The x-ray showed no fracture or dislocations. Dr. Shaw had seen Brandon for his school physical six months ago. Today, Dr. Shaw documented a detailed examination and decision-making of moderate complexity. He also instructed Brandon's mother that if Brandon had

any additional pain or trouble walking he should see an orthopedic specialist. How should Dr. Shaw report her services from today's visit?

a. 99204
b. 99394, 99214
c. 99214
d. 99203

41. Adam, a 48-year-old patient, presented to Dr. Crampon's office with complaints of fever, malaise, chills, chest pain, and a severe cough. Dr. Crampon took a history, did an exam, and ordered a chest x-ray. After reviewing the x-ray, Dr. Crampon admitted Adam to the hospital for treatment of pneumonia. After his regular office hours, Dr. Crampon visited Adam in the hospital where he dictated a comprehensive history, comprehensive examination, and decision-making of moderate complexity. How would you report Dr. Crampon's services?

a. 99214
b. 99222
c. 99204, 99222-51
d. 99223, 99214-24

42. Dr. Jane admitted a 67-year-old woman to the coronary care unit for an acute myocardial infarction. The admission included a comprehensive history, comprehensive examination, and high complexity decision making. Dr. Jane visited the patient on days two and three and documented (each day) an expanded problem focused examination and decision making of moderate complexity. On day four, Dr. Jane moved the patient to the medical floor and documented a problem focused examination and straight forward decision-making. Day five, Dr. Jane discharged the patient to home. The discharge took over an hour. How would you report the services from day one to day five?

a. 99213, 99232, 99231, 99239 x 2
b. 99221, 99222, 99223, 99238
c. 99231, 99232, 99355, 99217
d. 99223, 99232, 99232, 99231, 99239

Anesthesia

43. An anesthesiologist provides general anesthesia for a 72-year-old patient with mild systemic disease who is undergoing a ventral hernia repair. How would you report the anesthesia service?

a. 00834-P2, 99100
c. 49560, 00834, 99100-P2
b. 00832-P2, 99100
d. 00832-P2

44. A 44 year old patient is referred to a cardiologist because his pre admission EKG prior to surgery indicated that he may have had a heart attack on other heart injury in the past. The cardiologist, as part his assessment, performs an echocardiogram that does not confirm a previous heart injury, but does show a very small septal defect that physician documents as clinically in significant withy no treatment warranted. The cardiologist clears the patient for surgery. What is the proper code for this service?

a. 93306   b. 93307   c. 93303   d. 93304

45. Katherine is a 77-year-old patient with a severe hypertensive disease. She underwent a cataract surgery to both eyes under general anesthesia. Dr. Sharon, the anesthesiologist, performed the anesthesia. Prior to induction of anesthesia Dr. Sharon completed a preoperative visit and documented a detailed history, detailed examination, and low complexity decision-making on this new patient. How would you report Dr. Sharon's services?

a. 99203, 00142-P2, 99100
b. 66820, 00144
c. 00140-P1, 99116-59
d. 00142-P3, 99100

46. A surgeon performed a cervical approach esophagoplasty with repair of a tracheosophageal fistula under general anesthesia. The surgeon performed both the procedure and the anesthesia.
How would you report these services?
a. 00500, 43305
b. 43305-47
c. 00500-47
d. Both A and C

Radiology

47. Erin, a 45-year-old, asymptomatic female comes in for her annual bilateral screening mammography. Her physician ordered a computer aided detection along with the mammography. The procedure was performed in a hospital. How would you report the professional services for this study?
a. 77067-26
b. 7706-26
c. 77066-26
d. 77067

48. A patient presents to a freestanding radiology center and had ultrasonic guidance needle placement with imaging supervision and interpretation of two separate lesions in the left breast. The procedure required several passes to complete. How would you report the imaging procedure?
a. 76930 x 2
b. 76941
c. It is bundled with primary code
d. 76942 x 2-LT

49. Sally had a DXA bone density study for her hips,

pelvis, and spine. The procedure was performed in a hospital. How would you report for the professional services of this study?
a. 77078-26, 77080-26
b. 77080-26
c. 77082-26
d. 77081-26, 77080-26

50. How is proton beam treatment delivery defined?
a. Simple, Complex, and Compound
b. Simple, Complex, and Intermediate
c. Superficial, Deep Vein, and Distal
d. Simple, Complicated, and Comprehensive

51. A patient had a myocardial perfusion imaging, planar, single study at rest with quantification, ejection fraction, and wall motion study. The procedure was performed in the nuclear medicine department of the hospital. How would you report the professional services for this study?
a. 78473-26
b. 78451-26
c. 78452-26
d. 78453-26

52. Which of the following codes are unlisted procedures?
a. 76498, 78199, 76496, 77799
b. 75600, 75801, 76506, 76830
c. 74181, 74280, 75564, 75600
d. 75810, 75801, 75860, 75903

Pathology & Laboratory

53. Dr. Lee performed an intra-operative consultation on a bile duct tumor requiring frozen section and cytological evaluation to a bladder tumor. How would you report his professional services?

a. 88329	b. 88331-26, 88334-26
c. 88331, 88332 x 2	d. 88331-26, 88333-26

54. Marvin had a breath alcohol test completed at the hospital after the police arrested him for racing his four- wheeler past a McDonald's drive through window. Marvin's breath alcohol test was mathematically calculated. How would you report the calculation on this test?

a. 82075	b. 82075 x 2
c. 82075, 82355	d. 82355

55. Dr. Monday provided a comprehensive clinical pathology consultation at the request of Dr. Adams. This request was regarding a patient with various infections, drug allergies, skin rash, and Down's syndrome. The patient is in the hospital intensive care unit being treated with intravenous antibiotics. Dr. Monday did not see the patient but he reviewed the patient's history, complex medical records, and provided a written report back to Dr. Adams regarding his findings and recommendations for further treatment. How would Dr. Monday report his services?

a. 80502	b. 99244
c. 99244-25, 80502	d. 99255-25, 80500

56. A patient had a semi-quantitative urinalysis for infectious agent detection. How should you report this test?

a. 81050	b. 81005
c. 81007	d. 81005, 83518

57. A 58-year-old male patient with abdominal pain and episodes of bright red blood in his stool reports to his physician's office for a check-up. His physician performs a digital rectal exam and tests for occult blood.

Dr. Smith documents this blood occult test was done for purposes other than colorectal cancer screening. How would you report the occult blood test?

a. 82270 b. 82274
c. 82271 d. 82272

58. Kathy has had intermittent abdominal pain, occasional diarrhea, stool frequency, and bloating. Her symptoms have worsened over the past two months. Her physician orders a fecal Calprotectin test to check for Crohn's disease. How should you report the lab test?

a. 82270 b. 82272, 83993
c. 83993 d. 82271, 82272

Medicine

59. Colin had a comprehensive audiometry threshold evaluation and speech recognition testing to the left ear. What code(s) capture this procedure?

a. 92557-52 b. 92553, 92556
c. 92557 d. 92700-59

60. An adult patient had the following immunizations with administration: yellow fever vaccine, subcutaneous injection, Hepatitis B vaccine IM injection, Zoster (HZV) vaccine, subcutaneous. How would you report these services?

a. 90471, 90472 x 2, 90717-51, 90746-51, 90736-51
b. 90471, 90472 x 2, 90717, 90746, 90675
c. 90473, 90474 x 2, 90746, 90675, 90717
d. 90471, 90474 x 2, 90736-51, 90746-51, 90717-51

61. Sally suffered from dehydration after running a marathon. She was taken into her primary care doctor's office. Dr. small checked Sally and ordered hydra-

tion therapy with normal saline. The hydration lasted 45 minutes. How would you report this service?
a. 96365, 96361
b. 96369
c. 96360
d. 96360, 96361

62. A patient had a bronchoscopy with destruction for relief of stenosis by laser therapy. During this procedure photodynamic therapy by endoscopic application of light was used to ablate abnormal tissue via activation of photosensitive drugs. The photodynamic therapy lasted 60 minutes. How would you report this procedure?
a. 31645, 96567
b. 96567 x 2
c. 31643, 96570-51, 96571-51
d. 31641, 96570, 96571 x 2

63. Dr. George asked the local pharmacist to review Ann's new medications with her when she picked them up. Ann is a new patient who just moved into the area and required several new medications. Ann is hard of hearing and had a difficult time understanding Dr. George when he called her. The pharmacist spent 30 minutes with Ann and documented a review of her history, recommendations for improving health outcomes, and treatment compliance. The pharmacist faxed this note back to Dr. George's office. How would the pharmacist report his services?
a. 99605, 99607 x 2
b. 99605, 99607
c. 99607 x 3
d. 99213

64. PREOPERATIVE DIAGNOSIS: ATRIAL FIBRILLATION OPERATION DIRECT CURRENT CARDIOVERSION.

PROCEDURE: After obtaining informed consent a direct current cardioversion was performed. The patient was given sedation by a member of the anesthesia department. A 12000000000000 of synchronized shock was delivered but atrial fibrillation appeared to persist after a few sinus beats. Therefore, a 200 J of synchronized biphasic shock was delivered. Once again, sinus rhythm was restored but only for a few 50 seconds. Then, delivered a second 200 J of synchronized biphasic shock and then this time sinus rhythm was restored and persisted.

CONCLUSIONS: Successful direct current cardioversion after a few attempts with restoration of normal sinus rhythm. What is the first-listed CPT code for the patient encounter?

a. 92960
b. 96961
c. 92971
d. 92950

Terminology

65. In which part of the body would you find the choroid?
a. Brain
b. Eyeball
c. Muscles of the hand
d. Spinal column

66. Which combining form refers to the small intestine?
a. enter/o
b. gastr/o
c. celi/o
d. col/o

67. Which term refers to the anus, and the cecum?
a. Rectal
b. Anorectal

c. Esophageal   d. Ilium

68. Which term does not refer to a level of consciousness?
a. Syncope   b. Stupor
c. Coma   d. Sciatica

Anatomy

69. How can air pass through the upper respiratory tract?
a. Via nose, Nasal cavity, Nasopharynx, Oropharynx, and Larynx into the lower respiratory system.
b. Via the Nose, larynx, and bronchus
c. Via nose, larynx, bronchus, and trachea
d. Via nose, larynx, bronchus, trachea, pleuta

70. What is the uvula?
a. A receptable for urine before it is voided/
b. A female organ used to contain and nounsh the embryo and fetus from the time the fertilized egg is implanted to the time of birth of the fetus.
c. A small soft structure hanging from the free edge of the osoft palate in midline above the root of the tongue. It is composed of muscle, connective tissue, and mucous membrane.
d. A canal, used for the discharge of urine that extends from the bladder to the outside of the body.

71. What is the make up the axial skeleton?
a. Skull, ribcage and Spine
b. Spine, Collar bones, Arms
c. Shoulder bones, pelvic bones, arms and legs
d. Coccyx, ulna, femur and tibia

72. What term refers to white cells?
a. Erythrocytes   b. Monocytes
c. Lymphocytes   d. Leukocytes

Icd

73. A patient with AIDS is seen by her physician for severe dehydration. The final diagnosis by the physician is salmonella with dehydration. Code(s): ....
a. A02.8, B20
b. A02.9, B20
c. A02.9, Z
d. A02.8, Z21

74. Type 1 diabetic patient is brought to the ER by ambulance in a coma. Patient is pale, rapid heartbeat, and their face is covered in sweat. Physician finds the insulin pump not delivering insulin and after reviewing the lab's diagnosis the patient with diabetic ketoacidosis with diabetic coma.
a. T85.614A, T38.3X1A, E10.641
b. T85.614A, T38.3X6A, E10.11
c. E10.11, T85.614A, T38.3X6A
d. T85.614A, T38.3X6A, E11.641

75. Patient diagnosed with cellulitis of the abdominal wall and has an enterostomy infection.
a. L03.311
b. L03.911
c. K94.12, L03.311
d. K94.11

76. Patient is diagnosed with an ectopic pregnancy that is found to be in the fallopian tubes.
a. O00.9, Z3A.00
b. O00.0, Z3A.00
c. O07.0, Z3A.00
d. O00.1, Z3A.00

77. A patient presents to the nephrology clinic suffering from malignant hypertensive heart and stage V chronic kidney disease without heart failure, due to hypertension.

a. I13.11, I10   b. I13.11
c. I13.11, N18.5   d. N18.5, I10

Hcpcs

78. A patient received a 12 sq. cm. dermal tissue substitute of human origin, dermagraft. This treatment was completed due to a burn on the abdomen. How would you report the supply?

a. Q4107 x 12   b. Q4105 x 12
c. Q4106 x 12   d. Q4111 x 12

79. During an emergency room visit, Sally was diagnosed with pneumonia. She was admitted to the hospital observation unit and treated with 500 mg of Zithromax through an IV route. How would you report the supply of this drug?

a. J0456   b. Q0144
c. J1190 x 2   d. J2020 x 2

80. Alice had to have a replacement for her soft interface in her protective helmet. How would you report this supply?

a. A8004   b. A8000
c. A8001   d. A8002

Coding Guidelines

81. When using the CPT index to locate procedures, which of the following are considered primary classes for main entries?
   a. Procedure or service; organ or other anatomic site; condition; synonyms, eponyms, and abbreviations

b. Abbreviations; signs and symptoms, anatomic site; and code assignment
c. Conventions; code ranges; modifying terms
d. Procedure or service; modifiers; clinical examples; and definitions

82. How are the diagnoses sequenced when coding for multiple fractures?
a. Multiple fractures are sequenced according to anatomic location.
b. Multiple fractures are sequenced in accordance with the severity of the fracture.
c. Multiple fractures are sequenced in accordance with the longest bone first.
d. Multiple fractures are always sequenced with pathologic fractures.

83. When coding for a liver transplantation, what are the three distinct components of the physician's work?
a. Cadaver biopsy, cholecystectomy, reconstruction of the liver graft.
b. Cadaver/living donor hepatectomy, backbench work, recipient liver allotransplantation.
c. Preparations of the common bile duct, trisegment split management of liver hemorrhage with reexploration of post-operative abscess.
d. Hemorrhoidopexy, ligation and hepatectomy, cholecystectomy.

84. What statement is true when reporting pregnancy codes:
a. These codes can be used on the maternal and baby records.
b. These codes have sequencing priority over codes from other chapters.
c. Code O80.0 should always be reported with these codes.

d. The fifth digits assigned to these codes indicate the complication during the pregnancy.

85. Which of the following statements is true regarding sequencing of External cause codes?
a. External cause codes for place of occurrence take priority over all other External cause codes.
b. External cause codes for medical history take priority over all other external cause codes.
c. External cause codes identifying screening exam as the reason for encounter take priority over all other external cause codes.
d. External cause codes for transport accidents take priority over all other External cause codes except cataclysmic events and child and adult abuse and terrorism.

86. Physical status modifiers are appended to codes listed in which major section of the CPT book?
a. Evaluation and Management
b. Anesthesia
c. Surgery
d. Medicine

87. Panel tests in the pathology and laboratory section of the CPT book include all the codes listed with the panel description. When a panel is performed and additional Pathology/Laboratory tests are completed how should those additional tests be reported?
a. All tests are bundled when performed with a panel.
b. Reporting additional tests is up-coding and could flag an audit that always leads to financial penalties.
c. Both A and B
d. The additional test should be reported separately in addition to the panel code.

Compliance & Regulatory

88. Which of the following health plans does not fall under HIPAA?
a. Medicaid b. Medicare
c. Workers Compensation d. Private plans

89. What is PHI?
a. Physician-healthcare interchange
b. Private Health
c. Protected health information d. Patient health Information

90. Which of the following is a BENEFIT of electronic claims submission?
a. Privacy of claims
b. Security of claims
c. Timely submission of claims
d. None of the above

Case Scenario

91. PRE OP DIAGNOSIS: Left Breast Abnormal MMX or Palpable Mass; Other Disorders Of Breast
PROCEDURE: Automated Stereotactic Biopsy Left Breast

FINDINGS: Lesion is located in the lateral region, just at or below the level of the nipple on the 90 degree lateral view. There is a subglandular implant in place. I discussed the procedure with the patient today including risks, benefits and alternatives. Specifically discussed was the fact that the implant would be displaced out of the way during this biopsy procedure. Possibility of injury to the implant was discussed with the patient. Patient has signed the consent form and wishes to proceed with the biopsy. The patient was placed prone on the stereotactic table; the left breast was then imaged from the inferior approach. The lesion of interest is in the anterior portion of the breast away from the implant which was displaced back toward the chest wall. After imaging was obtained and stereotactic guidance used to target coordinates for the biopsy, the left breast was prepped with Betadine. 1% lidocaine was injected subcutaneously for local anesthetic. Additional lidocaine with epinephrine was then injected through the indwelling needle. The SenoRx needle was then placed into the area of interest. Under stereotactic guidance we obtained 9 core biopsy samples using vacuum and cutting technique. The specimen radiograph confirmed representative sample of calcification was removed. The tissue marking clip was deployed into the biopsy cavity successfully. This was confirmed by final stereotactic digital image and confirmed by post core biopsy mammogram left breast. The clip is visualized projecting over the lateral anterior left breast in satisfactory position. No obvious calcium is visible on the final post core biopsy image in the area of interest. The patient tolerated the procedure well. There were no apparent complications. The biopsy site was dressed with SteriStrips, bandage and ice pack in the usual manner. The patient did receive written and verbal postbiopsy instructions. The patient left our department in good condition.

IMPRESSION: 1. SUCCESSFUL STEREOTACTIC CORE BIOPSY OF LEFT BREAST CALCIFICATIONS. 2. SUCCESSFUL DEPLOYMENT OF THE TISSUE MARKING CLIP INTO THE BIOPSY CAVITY 3. PATIENT LEFT OUR DEPARTMENT IN GOOD CONDITION TODAY WITH POST-BIOPSY INSTRUCTIONS. 4. PATHOLOGY REPORT IS PENDING; AN ADDENDUM WILL BE ISSUED AFTER WE RECEIVE THE PATHOLOGY REPORT. What are the codes for the procedures?

A. 19081
B. 19081-26
C. 19081, 76942-26
D. 19081, 77012-26

92. PREOPERATIVE DIAGNOSIS: Diverticulitis, perforated diverticula POST OPERATIVE DIAGNOSIS: Diverticulitis, perforated diverticula

PROCEDURE: Hartman procedure, which is a sigmoid resection with Hartman pouch and colostomy. DESCRIPTION OF THE PROCEDURE: Patient was prepped and draped in the supine position under general anesthesia. Prior to surgery patient was given 4.5 grams of Zosyn and Rocephin IV piggyback. A lower midline incision was made, abdomen was entered.

Upon entry into the abdomen, there was an inflammatory mass in the pelvis and there was a large abscessed cavity, but no feces. The abscess cavity was drained and irrigated out. The left colon was immobilized, taken down the lateral perineal attachments. The sigmoid colon was mobilized. Therewas an inflammatory mass right at the area of the sigmoid colon consistent with a divertiliculitis or perforation with infection. Proximal to this in the distal left colon, the colon was divided using a GIA stapler with 3.5 mm staples. The sigmoid colon was then mobilized using blunt dissection. The proximal rectum just distal to the inflammatory mass was divided using a GIA stapler with 3.5 mm staples. The mesentary of the sigmoid colon was then taken down and tied using two 0 Vicryl ties. Irrigation was again performed and the sigmoid colon was removed with inflammatory mass. The wall of the abscessed cavity that was next to the sigmoid colon where the inflammatory mass was, showed no leakage of stool, no gross perforation, most likely there is a small perforation in one of the diverticula in this region. Irrigation was again performed throughout the abdomen until totally clear. All excess fluid was removed. The distal descending colon was then brought out through a separate incision in the lower left quadrant area and a large 10 mm 10 French JP drain was placed into the abscessed cavity. The sigmoid colon or the colostomy site was sutured on the inside using interrupted 3-0 Vicryl to the peritoneum and then two sheets of film were placed into the intra-abdominal cavity. The fascia was closed using a running #1 double loop PDS suture and intermittently a #2 nylon retention suture was placed. The colostomy was matured using interrupted 3-0 chromic sutures. I palpated the colostomy; it was completely patent with no obstructions.

Dressings were applied. Colostomy bag was applied.

Which CPT & ICD codes should be used?

A. 44140, K57.21
B. 44143, K57.20
C. 44160, K57.30
D. 44208, K57.20

93. PREOPERATIVE DIAGNOSIS: Right scaphoid fracture. TYPE OF PROCEDURE: Open reduction and internal fixation of right scaphoid fracture. DESCRIPTION OF PROCEDURE: The patient was brought to the operating room, anesthesia having been administered. The right upper extremity was prepped and draped in a sterile manner. The limb was elevated, exsanguinated, and a pneumatic arm tourniquet was elevated. An incision was made over the dorsal radial aspect of the right wrist. Skin flaps were elevated. Cutaneous nerve branches were identified and very gently retracted. The interval between the second and third dorsal compartment tendons was identified and entered. The respective tendons were retracted. A dorsal capsulotomy incision was made, and the fracture was visualized. There did not appear to be any type of significant defect at the fracture site. A 0.045 Kirschner wire was then used

as a guidewire, extending from the proximal pole of the scaphoid distalward. The guidewire was positioned appropriately and then measured. A 25-mm Acutrak drill bit was drilled to 25 mm. A 22.5-mm screw was selected and inserted and rigid internal fixation was accomplished in this fashion. This was visualized under the OEC imaging device in multiple projections. The wound was irrigated and closed in layers. Sterile dressings were then applied. The patient tolerated the procedure well and left the operating room in stable condition. What code should be used for this procedure?

A. 25628-RT, S62.001A   B. 25624-RT, S62.001A   C. 25645-RT, S62.009A   D. 25651-RT, S62.002A

94. PREOPERATIVE DIAGNOSIS: Medial meniscus tear, right knee

POSTOPERATIVE DIAGNOSIS: Medial meniscus tear, extensive synovitis with an impingement medial synovial plica, right knee

TITLE OF PROCEDURE: Diagnostic operative arthroscopy, partial medial meniscectomy and synovectomy, rightknee The patent was brought to the operating room, placed in the supine position after which he underwent general anesthesia. The right knee was then prepped and draped in the usual sterile fashion. The arthroscope was introduced through an anterolateral portal, interim portal created anteromedially. The suprapatellar pouch was inspected. The findings on the patella and the femoral

groove were as noted above. An intra-articular shaver was introduced to debride the loose fibrillated articular cartilage from the medial patellar facet. The hypertrophic synovial scarring between the patella and the femoral groove was debrided.

The hypertrophic impinging medial synovial plica was resected. The hypertrophic synovial scarring overlying the intercondylar notch and lateral compartment was debrided. The medial compartment was inspected. An upbiting basket was introduced to transect the base of the degenerative posterior horn flap tear. This was removed with a grasper. The meniscus was then further contoured and balanced with an intraarticular shaver, reprobed and found to be stable. The cruciate ligaments were probed, palpated and found to be intact. The lateral compartment was then inspected. The lateral meniscus was probed and found to be intact. The loose fibrillated articular cartilage along the lateral tibial plateau was debrided with the intra-articular shaver. The knee joint was then thoroughly irrigated with the arthroscope. The arthroscope was then removed. Skin portals were closed with 3-0 nylon sutures. A sterile dressing was applied. The patient was then awakened and sent to the recovery room in stable condition.

What CPT codes should be reported?

A. 29880-RT
B. 29881-RT
C. 29881-RT, 29822-59-RT
D. 29880-RT, 29822-59-RT

95. OPERATIVE NOTE

PREOPERATIVEDIAGNOSIS: Angina and coronary artery disease.

PROCEDURE DETAILS: The patient was brought to the operating room and placed in the supine position upon the table. After adequate general anesthesia, the patient was prepped with betadine soap and solution in the usual sterile manner. Elbow were protected to avoid ulnar neuropathy and phrenic nerve protectors were used to protect the phrenic nerve. All were removed at the end of the case.

A midline sternal skin incision was made and carried down through the sternum which was divided with the saw. Pericardial and thymus fat pad was divided. The left internal mammary artery was harvested and spatulated for anastomosis Heparin was given.

The Femoropoplteal vein was resected from the thigh, side branches secured using 4-0 silk and hemoclips. The thigh was closed multilayer vicryl and dexon technique. A pulsavac wash was done, drain was placed. The left internal mammary artery is sewn to the left anterior descending using 7-0 running prolene technique with the medtronc off-pump retractors. After this was done, the patient was fully heparinzed, cannulated with a 6.5 atrial cannula and a 2-stage venous catheter and begun on cardiopulmonary bypass and maintained normothemia. Medtronic retractors used to expose the circumflex. Prior to going on pump, we stapled the vein graft place to the aorta. Then on pump, we did the distal anastomosis with a 7-0 running prolene technique. The right side graft was brought to the posterior descending artery using running 7-0 prolene technique. Deairing procedure was carried out. The bulldog clamps were removed. The patient maintained good normal sinus rhythm with good mean perfusion. The patient was weaned from cardiopulmonary bypass. The arterial and venous lines were removed and doubly secured. Protamine was delivered. Meticulous hemostasis was present. Platelets were given for coagulopathy. Chest tube was placed and meticulous hemostasis was present. The anatomy and the flow in the grafts was excellent. Closure was begun. The sternum was closed with wire, followed by linea alba and pectus fascia closure with running 6-0 vicryl sutures in double-layer technique. The skin was closed with subcuticular 4-0 Dexon suture technique. The patient tolerated the procedure well and was transferred to the intensive care unit in stable condition.

a. 33510, 33533, 33572, I25.111

b. 33510, 33533, 35572, 32551, 36821, I25.111

c. 33533, 33517, 35572, I25.111

d. 35600, 35572, 33533, 33517, 32551, 36825, 33926, I25.111

96. The surgeon performed a tonsillectomy on a 25 year old male. Four hours after leaving the surgery center, the patient presents to the clinic with a 1 hour history of bleeding in the throat. The bleeding site was located; however, it was in a location that could not be treated outside the OR. The patient was taken back to the OR for control of postoperative bleeding. Code both procedures.
a. 42826,42961-78   b. 42831,42961-78
c. 42821,42961-58   d. 42836,42961-78

97. Preoperative Diagnosis:
Right colon cancer; probable liver metastasis Postoperative Diagnosis: Cecal cancer, extensive bilateral liver metastasis Procedures Performed: Right colectomy and biopsy of right lobe liver nodule

Indications: Patient is a 67-year-old man who presented with anemia. Colonoscopy demonstrated bleeding cecal carcinoma. CT scan suggested liver metastasis. He presents now for a palliative right colectomy and biopsy of liver nodule.

Description: The patient was brought to the operating room and placed in a supine position. Satisfactory general endotracheal anesthesia was achieved. He was prepped and draped exposing the anterior abdomen
and a lower midline incision was created sharply through subcutaneous tissues by electrocautery. Linea Alba was parted and exploration was performed. The right colon was mobilized by

dissection in the avascular plane. The patient had a three to four centimeter cecal cancer. The right ureter was identified and preserved.

The terminal ileum and distal ascending colon were divided with GIA-60 stapling devices. The right colic artery and lymph node tissue were resected back to the origin of the superior mesenteric artery with clamps and 3-0 silk ties. The specimen was forwarded to pathology. A stapled functional end-to-end anastomosis was then performed. The antimesenteric edges were reapproximated with a single fire of GIA-60 stapler. The defect created by the stapler was then closed with interrupted 3-0 silk Lembert sutures. The mesocolon was reapproximated with some interrupted 3-0 silk sutures. Hemostasis was confirmed. The right anterior liver nodule was biopsied with a needle. Hemostasis was achieved. The midline fascia was closed with running 1-0 Prolene suture. The skin was approximated with staples. The wound was dressed.

The procedure was concluded. The patient tolerated the procedure well and was taken to recovery in stable condition. Estimated blood loss was less than 100 cc. There were no complications.

Pathology Report
#1-Right Hemicolectomy: Adenocarcinoma of cecum
#2-Liver Biopsies: Metastatic adenocarcinoma. What additional information is needed from the operative report to assign a correct code?
What is/are the CPT Code(s)?
a. 44160, 47000-59
b. 44140, 47001-59
c. 44204, 47001-59
d. 44212, 47000-59

98. Preoperative Diagnosis: Left hydrocele Postoperative Diagnosis: Same

Operation Performed: Left hydrocelectomy

Indications: This 55-year-old male with a history of left hydrocele swelling causing discomfort requesting intervention after evaluation and preoperative consultation.

Operation: Patient was sterilely prepped and draped in the usual fashion. A transverse incision across the left hemiscrotum was made approximately 4 cm in length down to the level of the hydrocele. Hydrocele was removed from the incision and stripped of its fibrous attachments. Hydrocele was opened and drained. The excess sac was removed and discarded. The sac was then everted with the testicle, and a running #2-0 chromic stitch in a locking fashion was placed across the edges oft Meticulous hemostasis was achieved. The testicle and spermatic cord were then replaced back to the no damage done to the vas deferens. The dartos layer was reapproximated using #2-0 running locking chromic stitch. The skin was closed in a running horizontal mattress fashion using #3-0 chromic. The patient tolerated the procedure well.

What documentation from the operative report

is needed to accurately assign codes? What is/are

the CPT code(s)?

a. 55041, N43.3   b. 55500, N43.2

c. 55110, N43.2   d. 55040, N43.3

99. Preoperative Diagnosis: Uterine fibroids
Postoperative Diagnosis: Multiple uterine fibroids, uterus -250 g, 2 cm right ovarian cyst

Procedure:
Laparoscopic-assisted vaginal hysterectomy with bilateral salpingo-oophorectomy Procedure in Detail: The patient was taken to the operating room and placed in the supine position. After adequate general anesthesia had been obtained, the patient was prepped and draped in the usual fashion for laparoscopic-assisted vaginal hysterectomy. The bladder was drained. A small infraumbilical skin incision was made with the scalpel, and 10 mm laparoscopic sleeve and trocar were introduced without difficulty. The trocar was removed. The laparoscope was placed and 2 L of CO2 gas was insufflated in the patient's abdomen.

A second incision was made suprapubically and a 12-mm laparoscopic sleeve and trocar were introduced under direct visualization. A 5-mm laparoscopic sleeve and trocar were placed in the left lower quadrant under direct visualization. A manipulator was used to examine the patient's pelvic organs.

There was a small cyst on the right ovary. Both ovaries were free from adhesions. The ureters were free from the operative field. After measuring the ovarian distal pedicles, the endo-GIA staple was placed across each round ligament.

At this time, attention was turned to the vaginal part of the procedure. A weighted speculum was placed in the vagina. The anterior lip of the cervix was grasped with a Laheytenaculum. Posterior colpotomy incision was made and the posterior peritoneum entered in this fashion. The uterosacral ligaments were bilaterally clamped, cut, and Heaney sutured with #1 chromic.

The cardinal ligaments were bilaterally clamped, cut, and ligated. The anterior vaginal mucosa was then incised with the scalpel, and with sharp and blunt dissection, the bladder was freed from the underlying cervix. The bladder pillars were bilaterally clamped, cut, and ligated. The uterine vessels were then bilaterally clamped, cut, and ligated. Visualization was difficult because the patient had a very narrow pelvic outlet. In addition, several small fibroids made placement of clamps somewhat difficult. Using the clamp, cut, and tie method after the anterior peritoneum had been entered with scissors, the uterus was then left without vascular supply. The fundus was delivered by flipping the uterus posteriorly, and through an avascular small pedicle, Heaney clamps were placed across, and the uterus was then removed en bloc with the tubes and ovaries attached.

At this point, the remaining Heaney pedicles were ligated with a free-hand suture of 0 chromic. Sponge and instrument counts were correct. Avascular pedicles were inspected and found to be hemostatic. The posterior vaginal cuff was then, als usinging ranging interlocking suture of #1 chromic. The anterior peritoneum was then graspe de incoroscope pour frestring suture of O chromic, the peritoneum was closed. The paginal cuff was then closed reos feripiprating the previously tagged uterosacral ligaments into the vaginal cuff through the anterior and posterior vaginal cuff. Another figure-of-eight suture totally closed the cuff.

Hemostasis was excellent. Foley was then placed in the patient's bladder and clear urine was noted to be draining. At this point, the laparoscope was placed back through the 10-mm sleeve and the vaginal cuff inspected. A small amount of old blood was suctioned away, but all areas we hemostatic.

The laparoscopic instruments were removed after the excess gas had been allowed to escape. The incisions were closed first with suture of 2-0 Vicryl through the fascia of each incision, and then the skin edges were reapproximated with interrupted sutures of 3-0 plain. Sponge and instrument counts were correct. The patient was awakened from general anesthesia and taken to the recovery room in stable condition.

What key documentation is needed to lead to the correct coding range? What is/are the CPT Code(s)?

    a. 58542, D25.9   b. 58290, 58291, D25.9
    c. 58262, D25.9   d. 58260, 58262, D25

100. Preoperative Diagnosis; Recurrent acute serous otitis media on both ears. Postoperative Diagnosis: Same

Procedure: Bilateral myringotomy with ventilating tube insertion

Procedure in Detail: The patient was prepped and draped in the usual fashion under general anesthes Myringotomy was performed in the anterior-inferior quadrant and thick fluid suctioned from the middle e space. A Type I Paparella tube was then inserted. Then a myringotomy was performed on the left ear; again thick fluid was suctioned from the middle ear space. A Type I Paparella tube was then inserted.
CortisporinOtic Suspension drops were then placed in both ear canals and cotton in the ears. The pat was awakened and returned to the recovery room in satisfactory condition.
What coding guidance is provided in the textbook for this procedure? What is/are the CPT Code(s)?

a. 69421, 69436-50, H65.06

b. 69424, 69436-50, H65.06
c. 69421, 69433, H65.06
d. 69421, 69436, H65.111

Exam – 4

1. Stand-alone CPT codes have a full description; indented codes are listed under related stand-alone codes. An indented code includes the portion of the stand-alone code description, which precedes the semicolon. The semicolon is used in the CPT book to save space. Words following the semicolon can specify which of the following?
   a. Extent of the service, modifiers, specific anatomic site
   b. Extent of the service, specific anatomic site, unlisted services
   c. Extent of the service, specific anatomic site, alternative procedure
   d. Unlisted services, alternative procedures, specific anatomic site

2. Physical status modifiers are appended to codes listed in which major section of the CPT book?
   a. Evaluation and Management
   b. Anesthesia
   c. Surgery
   d. radiology

3. The term "intraservice time" has been measured in studies and is predictive of the work associated to E/M services. Intraservice times are defined as face-to-face time for office and other outpatient visits and as unit/floor time for hospital and other inpatient visits. What is included in the intraservice time for an office and other outpatient visits?

a. Time in which the physician obtains a history, performs an examination, provides patient counseling

b. Time in which the physician establishes/reviews the patient's chart and communicates with other professionals regarding the patient's family

c. Postoperative discussions, working with physical therapy departments, and counseling

d. Counseling/coordinating care that dominates more than 50% of the time with a patient

4. Panel tests in the Pathology and Laboratory section of the CPT book include all the codes listed with the panel description. When a panel is performed and additional

Pathology/laboratory tests are completed how should those additional tests be reported?

a. All tests are bundled when performed with a panel

b. Reporting additional tests is up-coding and could flag an audit that always leads to financial penalties

c. Both a and b

d. The additional test should be reported separately in addition to the panel code

5. A separate procedure is coded per CPT guidelines:
a. Is considered to be an integral part of a larger service.
b. Is coded when performed as a part of another larger procedure.
c. Is never coded under any circumstances.
d. Both a and b.

6. A bronchoscopy is
a. always a surgical procedure
b. always a diagnostic procedure
c. sometimes performed unilaterally or bilaterally
d. always performed bilaterally

7. True or false: A total abdominal hysterectomy and an oophorectomy performed within the same surgical session should be reported separately.
a. True   b. False

8. A patient presents for an incision and drainage of a pilonidal cyst. What is the correct code for these services?
a. 10060   c. 10080
b. 10061   d. 10081

9. A splinter is removed from the subcutaneous tissue of a patient's index finger through an incision made by the physician. The medical record states that this was a complicated procedure. How should the physician code this procedure?
a. 10121   c. 11010
b. 10120   d. 11011

10. On January 31st, Barbara had a two cm malignant lesion excised

from her left foot. During a postoperative check-up on February 2nd, a residual tumor was noted at the margin of the original excision and the margins were re-excised. The re-excision included a three cm excised diameter. How would the same physician code the re-excision?

a. 11622, 11623-59   c. 11623-59

b. 11626   d. 11623-58

11. Dr. Faye, a dermatologist specializing in Moh's, completed surgery on Howard's right thigh for an ill-defined skin cancer. Dr. Faye is acting as both the surgeon and pathologist for this surgery. The surgery consisted of nine excised specimens prepared and examined during stage one. Additionally, a total of seven excised specimens were prepared and examined during stage two. How would you code Dr. Faye's services?

a. 17311, 17312 x 6   c. 17313, 17314×6

b. 17313, 17314, 17315 x 6

d. 17311, 17312, 17315

12. A patient presents to the dermatologist's office to have six benign foot lesions removed. The dermatologist destroys these lesions by use of electrosurgery. How should the office code these services?

a. 17000, 17003-59   c. 17000, 17003 x 5

b. 17110   d. 17000, 17003

13. Gavin, a 39-year-old male patient, underwent a mastectomy for gynecomastia. His recovery was uneventful. What is the correct code to report the mastectomy?

a. 19300   c. 19307

b. 19302   d. None of the above

14. During a postpartum check-up, Kayla told Dr. Terry, her OBGYN, about a recurrent lump on her right wrist. Kayla has a history of

ganglion cysts on both wrists. Dr. Terry refers Kayla to Dr. Eagen, a general surgeon, who excises the cyst. How would you code Dr. Eagen's services?

a. 25112-RT

b. 26160

c. 25111

d. All services are included in postpartum care and should not be reported separately

15. What code(s) would be used to report the transfer of tendons to restore intrinsic function on all four fingers on the left hand with layered closure?

a. 26498, 12041   c. 26498 x 4

b. 26492   d. 26498-LT

16. Zachery injured his back while playing tennis; his injury required surgery. He was taken to the operating room where an orthopedic surgeon preformed an anterior osteotomy, including diskectomy to three thoracic vertebral segments. Additionally, Zachery required a structural bone graft obtained from a cadaver. How would you code this procedure?

a. 22222, 22226 x 2, 20931

b. 22226, 22222, 20931-51

c. 22216, 22212, 20938

d. 22212, 22216 x 2, 20938-51

17. Dr. Rami, an orthopedic surgeon, removed prosthesis from Cindy's left knee. Dr. Rami

inserted a spacer during the same surgery. How would you code for Dr. Rami's services? a. 27445-LT   c. 27331

b. 27310   d. 27488-LT

18. A patient has been diagnosed with Treacher-Collins Syndrome. A surgeon performs LeFortII to reconstruct the midface by anterior intrusion. How would you code for the surgeon's services?

a. 21150-22   c. 21150

b. 21141   d. 21151

19. Judy noticed swelling in both her hips. She is referred to Dr. Roy, an orthopedic surgeon, who performs a fasciotomy on both hips. Prior to surgery, Dr. Roy obtains the patient's permission to have a resident observe the surgery. What is the correct code for Dr. Roy's services?

a. 27025 x 2   c. 27025

b. 27025-50   d. 27025-80

20. Which code would be used to report a complete, primary, reshaping of the external nose with elevation of the nasal tip?

a. 30450   c. 30400

b. 30410   d. None of the above

21. Riley suffers from recurrent sinus infections. He underwent the following procedure to remove pus from the right sphenoid sinus. His physician entered the sphenoid sinus through the sphenoethmoidal recess in the superior nasal cavity. A flexible cannula was inserted into the opening and the right sinus was irrigated with saline solution. What is the correct code for this procedure?

a. 31002-RT   c. 31299

b. 31000-RT   d. 31002-50

22. True or false: The following coding combination 31526, 69990 are correct if reported together?

a. True   b. False

23. Polly had the battery changed for her single chamber permanent

pulse generator, which was inserted one year ago. This procedure was completed in the same session by the same provider. How should the provider's services be coded?

a. 33233, 33212-59   c. 33234, 33213-59

b. 33233, 33212-51   d. 33227

24. A physician performed an open biopsy of four deep cervical lymph nodes. How should the office code this service?

a. 38510 x 4   c. 38510

b. 57500   d. 38500

25. A physician performs a transluminal balloon angioplasty of the left iliac by inserting a catheter through the skin. The balloon is inflated several times during this procedure. The physician did not provide the radiological supervision and interpretation with this procedure. Which code indicates this service?

a. 37246   c. 37220, 37222

b. 37222   d. 37220

26. A patient presents with gastroesophageal reflux disease. To treat this disorder, the surgeon performs a laparoscopic Nissen procedure. A diagnostic laparoscopy was completed during the same session. What code(s) indicate this service?

a. 43280   c. 43325

b. 43289   d. 43280, 43325-52

27. A physician performs a V-excision of the lip with primary direct linear closure. This procedure was completed to remove a lesion. What code(s) describe these services?

a. 40510, 40520-51   c. 40510, 40525-51

b. 40520   d. 40530

28. A physician performs a Billroth II procedure, partial distal gastrectomy with gastrojejunostomy, and a vagotomy. Which codes capture these services?

a. 43631, 43635   c. 43632, 43635

b. 43631, 43635-51   d. 43632, 43635-51

29. Garret is diagnosed with ulcerative colitis. He is referred to a surgeon, Dr. Brown. He performs a continent ileostomy as treatment. What code(s) captures this service?

a. 44316   c. 44316, 44320-59

b. 44310   d. 44799

30. Dean lost his teeth in an auto accident one year ago. He has had several facial surgeries to restore his nasal function and rebuild the orbit of his eye and cheek. Currently, he is scheduled for a posterior complex vestibuloplasty with muscle repositioning. What code(s) capture the current procedure?

a. 40845   c. 40842, 40845

b. 40843-52   d. 40899

31. A physician inserts a catheter into a renal abscess under radiologic guidance. The physician then drains the abscess. The procedure was performed at the hospital. How should the physician's services be coded?

a. 49405   c. 49405, 75989-26

b. 49405-26   d. 49405, 75989

32. Mary underwent a bilateral vulvecomy with removal of 92% of the vulvar area. She also had an inguinofemoral lymphadenectomy dur-

ing the same operative session. What code(s) capture these services?

a. 56637-50   c. 56632
b. 56637   d. 56625, 38760

33. A physician performs laser vaporization of the prostate with a vasectomy. The patient had some postoperative bleeding that was controlled at the time of the procedure. What code(s) capture this service?

a. 52648   c. 52647-22
b. 52601, 52648-51 d. 52601, 54162-59

34. A patient had a percutaneous cryoabliaton of bilateral renal tumors. What code captures this service?

a. 53899
b. 50592 x 2
c. 50592-50
d. 50593-50

35. Cheryl is a 36-year-old established patient with Dr. Winn, an OBGYN. During Cheryl's annual physical examination, Dr. Winn noticed lesions on the perineum. After completing the annual exam, Dr. Winn biopsies five lesions on the perineum. How should his office code the service for the biopsy?

a. 56605, 56606 x 4   c. 56606, 56606-51
b. 99395, 56605, 56606 x 4
d. 99395, 56606, 56606-59

36. Mr. Bill has urinary incontinence. The urologist performs an anterior vesicourethropexy to correct the incontinence. The physician documented that this was a complicated repair.

What code captures this service?

a. 51840   c. 53440

b. 51841   d. 53899

37. Dr. Joyce performs a bilateral corpora cavernosa-saphenous vein shunt. Select the correct code(s) for this procedure.

a. 54420   c. 54420, 54420

b. 54420-50   d. 54430

38. Todd was in a motorcycle accident. He suffered multiple fractures and lacerations. During one surgical session, a surgeon elevated a depressed skull fracture. This procedure required repair of the dura. What code(s) capture these services?

a. 62010   c. 62005

b. 62000   d. 62005, 62010

39. A physician obtains corneal tissue from an eye bank and sizes the tissue for transplant. The physician then performs a lamellar keratoplasty. He removes the anterior layer of the diseased cornea and replaces it with the prepared donor tissue. What are the correct codes for these services?

a. 65710   c. 65757, 20926-62

b. 65755   d. 65710, 68371

40. A physician removed lens material for a cataract patient using an intracapsular technique and injected saline to restore intraocular pressure. What code(s) correctly capture these services?

a. 66930   c. 66920, 66020

b. 66920   d. 66930, 66020

41. Fred, a 45-year-old patient, suffered a profound hearing loss due to an industrial accident and had a cochlear device implanted without a mastoidectomy. The surgeon used an operating microscope during this procedure. What are the correct code(s) for this service?

a. 69930, 0072T   c. 69930, 69990

b. 69930-50   d. 69930, 69990-51

42. A physician repairs a retinal detachment by depressing a hot probe over the outer layer of the eyeball to seal the choroid to the retina. A scleral buckle is placed around the eyeball to support the healing scar. What code captures this service?

a. 67101   c. 67113

b. 67015   d. 67107

43. Two-year-old Bobby was running through the house with a Popsicle when he fell, suffering a three cm partial thickness laceration to his left upper eyelid. This injury involved the lid margin and tarsus. Bobby was taken to an emergency room by his parents and the physician did a direct layered closure. How would you code the physician's service?

a. 12052-E1   c. 67935-E1

b. 12002-LT   d. 67930-E1

44. Dr. Todd, a primary care physician, examines Keith for a cough producing phlegm, a low grade fever, and a headache. Keith has been a patient of Dr. Todd's for several years. Keith had knee surgery by an orthopedic surgeon less than a week ago. He was checked by his orthopedic surgeon one day ago and is healing well from the procedure. His surgeon suggested that he see his primary care physician regarding his other symptoms. Dr. Todd documents an expanded problem-focused history and examination, decision-making of low complexity, with a diagnosis of recurrent bronchitis. What code captures Dr. Todd's service?

a. 99213-24   c. 99213-59

b. 99214   d. 99213

45. Mr. Fisher was referred by his internist to a surgeon's office for a

consultation regarding hemorrhoids. The surgeon noted the request for consult in his medical record and sent a letter back to the referring physician. The surgeon completed a detailed history, detailed examination, and low decision-making. The surgeon recommended medical treatment and prescribed two different ointments and an oral medication. He suggested re- evaluation if the hemorrhoids caused Mr. Fisher problems in the future or if he continued to have active symptoms. What code correctly captures the surgeon's services?

a. 99243   c. 99203

b. 99241   d. 99214

46. A healthy 22-year-old female is seen for her annual examination. She is new to this clinic and this physician. She is taking no medication, has no family history of systemic disease, and states that she is smoking but trying to stop. During her annual exam she asks the physician to look at a mole on her upper right arm that has changed in appearance. The physician works up the mole, taking an additional problem-focused history, problem focused examination, and documenting straight-forward decision- making. The physician instructs her to watch the mole carefully and report any further changes. What code(s) correctly capture this encounter?

a. 99285   c. 99385, 99202-25

b. 99385, 99202   d. 99203

47. Donald's family requested a consultation for a second opinion with Dr. Polson, an oncologist. The family completed extensive research on the Internet and looked for an opinion regarding a new type of lung cancer treatment. Donald's current physician has recommended a surgical and chemotherapy treatment approach to the metastasis of the lung. Dr. Polson has not seen Donald in the past and evaluates him for throat and bilateral lung lesions. Dr. Polson documented a comprehensive examination, comprehensive history, and reviewed extensive management options, extensive data, and the high risk of complications and mortality. Dr.Polson spends 90 minutes face-to- face with the patient, then an additional 45 minutes with the patient and his family explaining their options. What codes correctly capture Dr. Pol-

son's services?

a. 99205, 99354   c. 99215, 99354-25

b. 99245, 99354   d. 99255-21

48. Lilly, a 36-year-old female, made an appointment to talk with her physician about prevention of sexually transmitted diseases including HIV. She saw the same physician three months ago for a complete physical. She is asymptomatic at this time but has engaged in some high-risk behavior. During this visit, Lilly discussed diagnostic and laboratory test results, family issues, substance abuse, and sexual practices. The visit lasted 30 minutes.

What code correctly captures this encounter?

This service is bundled with the next office visit

b. 99395

c. 99078

d. 99402

49. Dr. Parrish, a pediatrician, continues to follow Rachel, who is not critically ill but requires intensive cardiac and respiratory monitoring, frequent checks of her vital signs, nutritional adjustments, and oxygen monitoring. Rachel is 32-days-old with a current weight of 3,200 grams. Dr. Parrish saw Rachel three separate times on Tuesday. What code correctly captures Tuesday's services?

a. 99291   c. 99471 x 3

b. 99480   d. 99471

50. When does anesthesia time begin and end?

a. Time begins when the anesthesiologist begins to prepare the patient for the induction of anesthesia in the operating room or in an equivalent area. Time ends when the anesthesiologist is no longer in personal attendance and when the patient may be safely placed under postoperative supervision.

b. Time begins when the anesthesiologist begins to prepare the patient for induction of anesthesia in the operating room or chair side in a waiting area. Time ends when the patient can respond to simple questions.

c. Time begins when the anesthesiologist starts to prepare the patient for induction of anesthesia in the operating room or in an equivalent area. Time ends when the anesthesiologist leaves the operating room.

d. Time begins when the patient is considered "under" anesthesia and ends when the surgery site is closed.

51. An anesthesiologist administers general anesthesia to a one-year-old healthy patient undergoing a mediastinoscopy. What code(s) capture the anesthesia services?

a. 00528-P1, 99100   c. 00528

b. 00528, 99100-P1   d. 00528-P1

52. Anesthesia is administered, by an anesthesiologist, to a female patient with severe systemic disease. She is scheduled to deliver via Cesarean section. The anesthesia is for the delivery only. The delivery is uneventful with a healthy mother and baby at the end of the procedure. What code(s) correctly capture the anesthesia services?

a. 01961-P3   c. 01961-P2, 99100

b. 00850   d. 01962

53. A patient presents to the hospital with an embedded piece of wood in his left shoulder. The patient stated that he was cutting down a tree when a limb fell and punctured his shoulder. Dr. Weber, a surgeon, administered general anesthesia for removal of a foreign body to a patient shoulder. What code captures the surgeon's services?

a. 23330-22   c. 23330-47

b. 00450-P1   d. 00450-47

54. Dr. Jones owns the x-ray equipment in his office and serves as the employer to the technologist. He ordered a three-view film of Paula's zygomatic bone. He reviewed the films and dictated a report while she was in the office. What code captures Dr. Jones' services?

a. 70150-26   c. 70150-TC

b. 70150   d. 70150-52

55. Dr. White ordered an MRI of Jerry's pelvis without contrast. Jerry went to the local outpatient imaging center for this study. The MRI was completed and read by a radiologist at the imagining center. A complete report was sent back to Dr. White. What code captures the radiology service?

a. 72196   c. 72195-26

b. 72195   d. 72198

56. Becky reported to her physician's office after feeling a lump in her right breast. Dr. Sarah had the results of Becky's last screening mammography, which did not show any changes. Dr.Sarah completed an exam and detected a lump in the right breast and abnormal changes in the left breast. After a complete work-up Dr. Sarah ordered a bilateral diagnostic mammography with computer aided detection. What code(s) correctly capture the mammography?

a. 77067, 77062   c. 77067, 77063

b. 77066   d. 77067

57. Mr. Fredrick is in his second phase of radiation treatment for stomach cancer. Today, he reports to the cancer treatment facility for his regularly scheduled treatment. He is given seven MeV to a single area that requires a single port and a simple block. How should the facility report this service?

a. 77412   c. 77417

b. 77402   d. 77402-TC

58. Tiffany is pregnant with twins after a successful IVF treatment. She is in her first trimester of pregnancy. Her physician completed a transabdominal follow-up ultrasound to evaluate the fetal size of both babies and review a suspected abnormality from a previous ultrasound. What code(s) correctly capture this service?

a. 76816, 76816-59   c. 76801, 76802 x 2

b. 76816 x 2   d. 76811, 76812

59. What code best describes a CT scan of the abdomen with oral contrast?

a. 74175   c. 74150

b. 74170   d. 74160

60. Dr. Bob verbally requested Dr. Heinz, a clinical pathologist, to provide a consultation for one of his patients. Dr. Heinz provided a comprehensive consultation with review of the patient's history, medical records, and sent a written report back to Dr. Bob. Which code correctly captures Dr. Heinz's services?

a. 80502   c. 88323

b. 88321   d. 99255

61. Dr. Shaw performed an electrolyte panel on automated equipment in her office. The tests she includes in this battery are sodium, potassium, chloride, carbon dioxide, and glucagon tolerance test. How should she report these services?

a. 82374, 82435, 84132, 84295, 82946

b. 80051, 82946

c. 80051

d. 80053-52

62. A patient presents to the hospital for a scheduled procedure

to remove suspicious lesions from the right side of her neck. The surgeon excised one lesion near the anterior portion of the mandible, the second near the clavicle bone. A pathologist received two separately labeled containers, container A-mandible, and container B-clavicle. The surgeon requests a consult during surgery for immediate diagnosis. The pathologist examines each specimen, taking two blocks from specimen A and three blocks from specimen B. Specimen A is further processed into two frozen sections and B into five frozen sections. The blocks are examined microscopically. What codes correctly capture the pathologist's services?

a. 88331, 88332-26 x 2

b. 88331 x 2, 88332 x 5

c. 88331, 88332 x 7

d. 88329, 88331-47, 88332-26 x 2

63. A 22-year-old female presents in the emergency department in a coma. Her friends tell the attending physician they were drinking and saw her take a couple of pills before she passed out. She has a history of depression and anxiety and is being treated with prescription medication. The physician orders a drug screen for alcohol, tricyclic antidepressants, opiates, and barbiturates. The lab completes a single drug class screening for each analyte by means of immunoassay methods. What code(s) correctly capture the lab services?

a. 80307 x 4   c. 80305 x 4

b. 80307   d. 80305

64. Dr. Kim performed a fine needle aspiration of deep tissue under radiological guidance. Two specimens were sent to the hospital laboratory for cytopathology evaluation to determine adequacy of the specimens gathered. What code(s) correctly capture the lab services?

a. 88173   c. 88173, 88333-91

b. 88172   d. 88712 x 2, 88334-59

65. A breast lesion was submitted for surgical pathology gross and microscopic evaluation of the surgical margins. A comprehensive consultation was done and report was completed with review of records and specimens. What code(s) correctly capture the laboratory services?

a. 88307   c. 88305

b. 88307, 88325-26   d. 88305, 88325-26

66. Mr. North presented for his weekly therapeutic visit with his physician. During this visit Mr. North had a comprehensive computer-based motion analysis study with videotaping and 3-D kinematicis, with dynamic plantar pressure measurements during walking. This study was completed to assist with major therapeutic decision-making for continued gait training and rehabilitation after a stroke. What code(s) should correctly capture this procedure?

a. 96001   c. 97116

b. 99214, 96000   d. 97116, 96001-59

67. Dr. Edit preformed a percutaneous left heart catheterization with injection procedures for coronary angiography and left ventriculography. Dr. Edit also completed the imaging supervision interpretation and report. This procedure was completed in a hospital setting.

How should Dr. Edit code his services? a. 93458   c. 93458-26

b. 93452, 93454-26   d. 93452

68. Jeffery, a six-year-old established patient, was given a measles, mumps, rubella, and varicella (MMRV) vaccination. This vaccination was completed the same day as his regularly scheduled annual pediatric checkup. The physician completed all necessary paperwork and examination for Jeffery. The physician provided face-to-face counseling with Jeffery's mother, while she was in the exam room with Jeffrey. The physician stayed in the exam room during the vaccine administration to continue to answer questions. What codes correctly capture the physician's services?

a. 99393, 90710, 90460, 90461x3

b. 90707, 90460

c. 99393, 90710, 90460x4

d. 90710, 90461

69. Joe, a 42-year-old construction worker, had hot packs applied to his knee and elbow and ultrasound for 30 minutes. He is scheduled to have eight physical rehabilitation sessions to help eliminate pain in his knee and elbow suffered when he fell from a ladder. This is his second visit and reports some relief. What codes correctly capture these services?

a. 97010 x 2, 97035   c. 97014, 97035

b. 97010, 97035 x 2   d. 97010 x 2, 97035×2

70. Madison was attending a soccer camp when she complained of fatigue, dizziness, and a headache. Her mother took her to Dr. Boyle's office for a checkup that afternoon. Dr. Boyle completed an expanded problem-focused history and examination, and then determined that Madison was dehydrated. Madison received five hours of IV infusion. What codes capture these services?

a. 96360, 96361 x 5

b. 96360, 96361

c. 96360, 96361 x 4

d. 99203, 96360 x 2, 96361 x 4

71. A patient with known hearing loss in the left ear presents for an audiometry threshold function test with speech recognition. Calibrated electronic equipment is used for this testing procedure. What code(s) capture this procedure?

a. 92557-22, 69990   c. 92555-47

b. 92552-50, 69990   d. 92556-52

72. During a cheiloplasty, the physician is repairing what part of the body?

The cervix   c. The cecum

The lip   d. The liver

73. What procedure involves the destruction of kidney stones by directing shock waves through liquid surrounding the patient?

a. Cystourethroscopy

b. Transurethral resection

c. Lithotripsy

d. Contact laser vaporization

74. Which suffix means blood or blood condition?

a. emia   c. penia

b. oma   d. uria

75. What term refers to toward or nearer the midline?

a. Ventral   c. Dorsal

b. Distal   d. Medial

76. Which term describes a type of fracture?

Greenstick   c. Depressed

Comminuted   d. All of the above

77. Which lung has three lobes?

Left lung   b. Right lung

78. The nervous system can be grouped into what two major categories?

a. Parasympathetic and sympathetic nervous systems

b. Somatic and norepinephrine nervous systems

c. Efferent and peripheral nervous systems

d. Central and peripheral nervous systems

79. True or false: The pineal gland is found in the brain near the thalamus and produces the hormone melatonin, which assists with sleep patterns.

True   b. False

80. Roger, a firefighter, was burned while fighting a forest fire. He is being treated in a burn unit, with burns to 30% of his total body surface area. The burns are reported as third degree to 25% of his body. The remaining 5% are first- and second-degree burns of the upper limb.

How should you report the diagnoses codes?

a. T31.32, T22.20XA, T22.10XA, X01.8XXA

b. T22.20XA. T31.31, X01.08XA

c. T31.32, T22.20XA, X01.8XXA

d. T31.31, T22.20XA, T22.10XA, X01.8XXA

81. Karen, a 26-year-old healthy female, suffered a cardiac arrest with administration of anesthetic during delivery. What are the correct diagnoses codes?

a. O74.2, I46.9   c. O74.4, I46.9

b. I46.9, O74.2   d. O74.9, I46.9

82. Thomas was seen in his primary care physician's office for a chronic smoker's cough. Thomas currently smokes five packs of cigarettes per day but is trying to quit smoking.

Dr. Smith notes a chest x-ray reveals abnormal changes in his left lower lobe and designates "rule out lung cancer" as a working diagnosis. How should Dr. Smith report the diagnoses for this visit?

a. J41.0, F17.211, R91.8

b. C34.30, F17.211

c. C34.32, F17.218

d. J41.0, F17.211

83. Today, Dr. Arnold is treating Harry for a sprained ankle and foot. Harry injured himself when he fell off a sidewalk curb at a local restaurant. Harry has HIV and is stable on his current medications. How would Dr. Arnold report the diagnoses for this visit?

a. B20, S93.409A, S93.609A, W10.1XXA, Y92.511

b. S93.409A, S93.609A, B20, W10.1XXA, Y92.511

c. Z21, S93.409A, S93.609A, W10.1XXA, Y92.511

d. Z21, S93.409A, W10.1XXA, Y92.29

84. Sherri presents for her regularly scheduled chemotherapy and radiation treatment. She is being treated for cancer in situ of the bladder wall. How would you list the diagnoses codes for this visit?

a. D30.3, Z51.1, Z51.0

b. C67.9, Z51.0

c. Z51.0, Z51.11, D09.0

d. D09.0, Z51.11, Z51.0

85. Bryce was burned on his left upper arm and requires a graft of nine sq. cm of tissue. He is being treated with dermal and epidermal tissue substance of human origin, Apligraft. What HCPCS Level II code should you report?

a. Q4101x 9   c. Q4106 x 7

b. J7330   d. Q4101 x 4

86. A 75-year-old patient with a history of malignant neoplasm of the

lower gastrointestinal trace presents for his follow-up colorectal cancer screening. Today, he has a colonoscopy.

What HCPCS Level II code describes this procedure?

a. G0104   c. G0120

b. G0105   d. G0121

87. Jose injured his eye while building a fence in his backyard. He sees his physician and is told to keep his eye covered while it heals. The physician gave him five sterile eye pads. What is the correct HCPCS Level II code for the eye pads?

a. A6411   c. A6410 x 5

b. A6411 x 5   d. A6410

88. Which of the following health plans does not fall under HIPAA?

A. Medicaid

B. Medicare

C. Workers' compensation

D. Private plans

89. What tool is in place that manages multiple third-party payments to ensure that over-payment does not happen?

a. FUD

b. DME

c. COB

d. PRO

90.. A PAR provider:

a. signs an agreement with the Fiscal Intermediary(Insurance)

b. submits charges directly to CMS

c. receives 5% less than some other providers

d. can bill the patient after payment from Medicare.

91. OPERATIVE REPORT

Preoperative Diagnosis: Basal Cell Carcinoma Postoperative Diagnosis: Basal Cell Carcinoma Location: Mid Parietal Scalp Procedure:

Prior to each surgical stage, the surgical site was tested for anesthesia and re-anesthetized as needed, after which it was prepped and draped in a sterile fashion. The clinically-apparent tumor was carefully defined and de-bulked prior to the first stage, determining the extent of the surgical excision. With each stage, a thin layer of tumor-laden tissue was excised with a narrow margin of normal appearing skin, using the Moh's fresh tissue technique. A map was prepared to correspond to the area of skin from which it was excised. The tissue was prepared for the cryostat and

sectioned. Each section was coded, cut and stained for microscopic examination. The entire base and margins of the excised piece of tissue were examined by the surgeon. Areas noted to be positive on

the previous stage (if applicable) were removed with the Moh's technique and processed for analysis. No tumor was identified after the final stage of microscopically controlled surgery. The patient tolerated the procedure well without any complication. After discussion with the patient regarding the various options, the best closure option for each defect was selected for optimal functional and cosmetic results. Preoperative Size: 1.5 x 2.9 cm

Postoperative Size: 2.7 x 2.9 cm

Closure: Simple Linear Closure, 3.5cm, scalp Total # of Moh's Stages: 2

Stage Sections Positive I- 6 blocks

II- 2 blocks

92. Operative Report

PREOPERATIVE DIAGNOSIS: Squamous cell carcinoma, scalp. POSTOPERATIVE DIAGNOSIS: Squamous carcinoma, scalp.

PROCEDURE PERFORMED: Excision of Squamous cell carcinoma, scalp with Yin-Yang flap repair ANESTHESIA: Local, using 4 cc of 1% lidocaine with epinephrine.

COMPLICATIONS: None.

ESTIMATED BLOOD LOSS: Less than 5 cc.

SPECIMENS: Squamous cell carcinoma, scalp sutured at 12 o'clock, anterior tip

INDICATIONS FOR SURGERY: The patient is a 43-year-old white man with a biopsy-proven basosquamous cell carcinoma of his scalp measuring 2.1 cm. I marked the area for excision with gross normal margins of 4 mm and I drew my planned Yin-Yang flap closure. The patient observed these markings in two mirrors, so he can understand the surgery and agreed on the location and we proceeded.

DESCRIPTION OF PROCEDURE: The area was infiltrated with local anesthetic. The patient was placed prone, his scalp and face were prepped and draped in sterile fashion. I excised the lesion as drawn to include the galea. Hemostasis was achieved with the Bovie cautery. Pathologic analysis showed the margins to be clear. I incised the Yin-Yang flaps and elevated them with the underlying galea.

Hemostasis was achieved in the donor site using Bovie cautery. The flap rotated into the defect with total measurements of 2.9 cm x 3.2 cm. The donor sites were closed and the flaps inset in layers using 40 Monocryl and the skin stapler. Loupe magnification was used. The patient tolerated the procedure well. What CPT® and ICD-10-CM codes are reported?

93.Operative Report

PREOPERATIVE DIAGNOSIS: Diabetic foot ulceration. POSTOPERATIVE DIAGNOSIS: Diabetic foot ulceration.

OPERATION PERFORMED: Debridement and split thickness autografting of left foot ANESTHESIA: General endotracheal.

INDICATIONS FOR PROCEDURE: This patient with multiple complications from Type II diabetes has developed ulcerations which were debrided and homografted last week. The homograft is taking quite nicely; the wounds appear to be fairly clean; he is ready for autografting.

DESCRIPTION OF PROCEDURE: After informed consent the patient is brought to the operating room and placed in the supine position on the operating table. Anesthetic monitoring was instituted, internal anesthesia was induced. The left lower extremity is prepped and draped in a sterile fashion. Staples were removed and the homograft was debrided from the surface of the wounds. One wound appeared to have healed; the remaining two appeared to be relatively clean. We debrided this sharply with good bleeding in all areas. Hemostasis was achieved with pressure, Bovie cautery, and warm saline soaked sponges. With good hemostasis a donor site was then obtained on the left anterior thigh, measuring less than 100 cm2. The wounds were then grafted with a split-thickness autograft that was harvested with a patch of Brown dermatome set at 12,000 of an inch thick. This was meshed 1.5:1. The donor site was infiltrated with bupivacaine and dressed. The skin graft was then applied over the wound, measured approximately 60 cm2 in dimension on the left foot. This was secured into place with skin staples and was then dressed with Acticoat 18's, Kerlix incorporating a catheter, and gel pad. The patient tolerated the procedure well. The right foot was redressed with skin lubricant sterile gauze and Ace wrap. Anesthesia was reversed. The patient was brought back to the ICU in satisfactory condition. What CPT® and ICD-10-CM codes are reported?

94. Operative Report

Diagnosis: Basal Cell Carcinoma

Procedure: Moh's micrographic excision of skin cancer. Site: face left lateral canthus eyelid

Pre-operative size: 0.8 cm

Indications for surgery: Area of high recurrence, area of functional and/or cosmetic importance Discussed procedure including alternative therapy, expectations, complications, and the possibility of a larger or deeper defect than expected requiring significant reconstruction. Patient's questions were answered.

Local anesthesia 1:1 marcaine and 1% lidocaine with epinephrine. Sterile prep and drape.

Stage 1: The clinically apparent lesion was marked out with a small rim of normal appearing tissue and excised down to subcutaneous fat level with a defect size of 1.2 cm. Hemostasis was obtained and a pressure bandage placed. The tissue was sent for slide preparation. Review of the slides show clear margins for the site.

Repair: Complex repair.

Repair of Moh's micrographic surgical defect. Wound margins were extensively undermined in order to mobilize tissue for closure. Hemostasis was achieved. Repair length 3.4 cm. Narrative: Burrows triangles removed anteriorly (medial) and posteriorly (lateral). A layered closure was performed. Multiple buried absorbable sutures were placed to re-oppose deep fat. The epidermis and dermis were re-opposed using monofilament sutures. There were no complications; the patient tolerated the procedure well.

Post-procedure expectations (including discomfort management), wound care and activity restrictions were reviewed. Written Instructions with urgent contact numbers given, follow-up visit and suture removal in 3-5 days

What CPT® and ICD-10-CM codes are reported?

95. A patient is seen in the same day surgery unit for an arthroscopy to remove some loose bodies in the shoulder area. What CPT® code(s) should be reported?

96. PRE OP DIAGNOSIS: Left Breast Abnormal MMX or Palpable Mass; Other Disorders Of Breast PROCEDURE: Automated Stereotactic Biopsy Left Breast FINDINGS: Lesion is located in the lateral region, just at or below the level of the nipple on the 90 degree lateral view. There is a subglandular

implant in place. I discussed the procedure with the patient today including risks, benefits and alternatives. Specifically discussed was the fact that the implant would be displaced out of the way during this biopsy procedure. Possibility of injury to the implant was discussed with the patient.

Patient has signed the consent form and wishes to proceed with the biopsy. The patient was placed prone on the stereotactic table; the left breast was then imaged from the inferior approach. The lesion of interest is in the anterior portion of the breast away from the implant which was displaced back toward the chest wall. After imaging was obtained and stereotactic guidance used to target coordinates for the biopsy, the left breast was prepped with Betadine. 1% lidocaine was injected subcutaneously for local anesthetic. Additional lidocaine with epinephrine was then injected through the indwelling needle. The SenoRx needle was then placed into the area of interest. Under stereotactic guidance we obtained 9 core biopsy samples using vacuum and cutting technique. The specimen radiograph confirmed representative sample of calcification was removed. The tissue marking clip was deployed into the biopsy cavity successfully. This was confirmed by final stereotactic digital image and confirmed by post core biopsy mammogram left breast. The clip is visualized projecting over the lateral anterior left breast in satisfactory position. No obvious calcium is visible on the final post core biopsy image in the area of interest. The patient tolerated the procedure well. There were no apparent complications. The biopsy site was dressed with SteriStrips, bandage and ice pack in the usual manner. The patient did receive written and verbal postbiopsy instructions. The patient left our department in good condition. IMPRESSION: 1. SUCCESSFUL STEREOTACTIC CORE BIOPSY OF LEFT BREAST CALCIFICATIONS. 2. SUCCESSFUL DEPLOYMENT OF THE

TISSUE MARKING CLIP INTO THE BIOPSY CAVITY 3. PATIENT LEFT OUR DEPARTMENT IN GOOD CONDITION TODAY WITH POST-BIOPSY INSTRUCTIONS. 4. PATHOLOGY REPORT IS PENDING; AN ADDENDUM WILL BE ISSUED AFTER WE RECEIVE THE PATHOLOGY REPORT. What are the codes for

the procedures?

97. EMERGENCY DEPARTMENT REPORT CHIEF COMPLAINT: Nasal bridge laceration.

SUBJECTIVE: The patient is a 74-year-old male who presents to the emergency department with a laceration to the bridge of his nose. He fell in the bathroom tonight. He recalls the incident. He just sort of lost his balance. He denies any vertigo. He denies any chest pain or shortness of breath. He denies any head pain or neck pain. There was no loss of consciousness. He slipped on a wet floor in the bathroom and lost his balance; that is how it happened. He has not had any blood from the nose or mouth.

PAST MEDICAL HISTORY: Parkinson's, Back pain, Constipation MEDICATIONS: See the patient record for a complete list of medications.

ALLERGIES: NA.

REVIEW OF SYSTEMS: Per HPI. Otherwise, negative.

PHYSICAL EXAMINATION: The exam showed a 74-year-old male in no acute distress. Examination of the HEAD showed no obvious trauma other than the bridge of the nose, where there is approximately a 1.5- to 2-cm laceration. He had no bony tenderness under this. Pupils were equal, round, and reactive. EARS and NOSE: OROPHARYNX was unremarkable. NECK was soft and supple. HEART was regular. LUNGS were clear but slightly diminished in the bases.

PROCEDURE: The wound was draped in a sterile fashion and anesthetized with 1% Xylocaine with sodium bicarbonate. It was cleansed with sterile saline and then repaired using interrupted 6-0 Ethilon sutures (Dr. Barney Teller, first-year resident, assisted with the suturing).

ASSESSMENT: Nasal bridge laceration, status post fall.

Plan: Keep clean. Sutures out in 5 to 7 days. Watch for signs of infection.

98. OPERATIVE REPORT

PREOPERATIVE DIAGNOSIS: Leaking from intestinal anastomosis.
POSTOPERATIVE DIAGNOSIS: Leaking from intestinal anastomosis.

PROCEDURE PERFORMED: Proximal ileostomy for diversion of colon. Oversew of right colonic fistula.

OPERATIVE NOTE: This patient was taken back to the operating room from the intensive care unit. She was having acute signs of leakage from an anastomosis I performed 3 days previously. We took down some of the sutures holding the wound together. We basically exposed all of this patient's intestine. It was evident that she was leaking from the small bowel as well as from the right colon. I thought the only thing we could do would be to repair the right colon. This was done in two layers, and then we freed up enough bowel to try to make an ileostomy proximal to the area of leakage. We were able to do this with great difficulty, and there was only a small amount of bowel to be brought out. We brought this out as an ileostomy stoma, realizing that it was of questionable viability and that it should be watched closely. With that accomplished, we then packed the wound and returned the patient to the intensive care unit.

99. OPERATIVE REPORT PREOPERATIVE DIAGNOSIS: Fever.

PROCEDURE PERFORMED: Lumbar puncture.

DESCRIPTION OF PROCEDURE: The patient was placed in the lateral decubitus position with the left side up. The legs and hips were flexed into the fetal position The lumbosacral area was sterilely prepped. It was then numbed with 1% Xylocaine. I then placed a 22-gauge spinal needle on the first pass into the intrathecal space between the L4 and L5 spinous processes. The fluid was minimally xanthochromic. I sent the fluid for cell count for differential, protein, glucose, Gram stain, and culture. The patient tolerated the procedure well without apparent complication. The needle was removed at the end of the procedure. The area was cleansed, and a Band-Aid was placed.

100. OPERATIVE REPORT

OPERATIVE PROCEDURE: Excision of back lesion.

INDICATIONS FOR SURGERY: The patient has an enlarging lesion on the upper midback. FINDINGS AT SURGERY: There was a 5-cm, upper midback lesion.

OPERATIVE PROCEDURE: With the patient prone, the back was prepped and

draped in the usual sterile fashion. The skin and underlying tissues were anesthetized with 30 mL of 1% lidocaine with epinephrine.

Through a 5-cm transverse skin incision, the lesion was excised. Hemostasis was ensured. The incision was closed using 3-0 Vicryl for the deep layers and running 3-0 Prolene subcuticular stitch with Steri-Strips for the skin.

The patient was returned to the same-day surgery center in stable postoperative condition. All sponge, needle, and instrument counts were correct. Estimated blood loss is 0 mL.

PATHOLOGY REPORT LATER INDICATED: Dermatofibroma, skin of back. Assign code(s) for the physician service only.

Exam - 5

Coding Guidelines

1. Specific coding guidelines in the CPT manual are located in the:
   a. Index.
   b. Introduction.
   c. Beginning of each section.
   d. Appendix A.

2. Which HCPCS modifier indicates the great toe of the right foot?
   a. T1
   b. T3
   c. T4
   d. T5

3. Which punctuation mark between codes in the index of the CPT manual indicates a rangeof codes is available?
   a. period
   b. comma
   c. semicolon
   d. hyphen

4. Staged or related procedure or service by the same physician during the postoperative-period
   a. 99
   b. 52
   c. 58
   d. 62

5. Anesthesia serviceincludes the following care

a. Preoperative, intraoperative

b. Preoperative, intraoperative,

c. postoperativeIntraoperative,

d. postoperative Preoperative, postoperative

6. The term that indicates this is the type of code for which the full code description can beknown only if the common part of the code (the description preceding the semicolon) ofa preceding entry is referenced:
   a. stand-alone   c. independent
   b. indented   d. add-on

7. If the anesthesia service were provided to a patient who had severe systemic disease, what would the physical status modifier be?
   a. P1   c. P3
   b. P2   d. P4

Integumentary System

8. What code would be used to code the destruction of a malignant lesion on the genitaliameasuring 1.6 cm using cryosurgery?
   a. 17272   c. 11420
   b. 11602   d. 11622

9. The patient is brought to surgery for an open wound of the left thigh, the total extentmeasuring approximately 40 x35CM
DESCRIPTION OF PROCEDURE: The legs were prepped with Betadine scrub and solution and then draped in a routine sterile fashion. Split-thickness skin grafts measuring about a 10,000th inch thick were taken from both thighs, meshed with a 3:1 ratio mesher, and stapled to the wounds. The donor sites were dressed with scarlet red, and the recipient sites were dressed with Xeroform,

Kerlix fluffs, and Kerlix roll, and a few ABD pads were used for absorption. Estimated blood loss was negligible. The patient tolerated the procedure well and left surgery in good condition. 35 cm.

    a. 15120, 15121 x 12
    b. 15100, 15101, 11010
    c. 15220, 15221 x 13
    d. 15100, 15101 x 13

10. SAME-DAY SURGERY
DIAGNOSIS: Inverted nipple with mammary duct ectasia, left. OPERATION: Excision of mass deep to left nipple.
With the patient under general anesthesia, a circumareolar incision was made with sharp dissection and carried down into the breast tissue. The nipple complex was raised up using a small retractor. We gently dissected underneath to free up the nipple entirely. Once this was done, we had the nipple fully unfolded, and there was some evident mammary duct ectasis. An area 3 x 4 cm was excised using electrocautery. Hemostasis was maintained with the electrocautery, and then the breast tissue deep to the nipple was reconstructed using sutures of 3-0 chromic. Subcutaneous tissue was closed using 3-0 chromic, and then the skin was closed using 4-0 Vicryl. Steri-Strips were applied. The patient tolerated the procedure well and was returned to the recovery area in stable condition. At the end of the procedure, all sponges and instruments were accounted for.

    a. 19120-RT
    b. 11404-LT
    c. 19112
    d. 19120-LT

11. What code(s) is used by the radiologist when performing preoperative placement of aneedle localization wire of a single lesion of the breast using MRI guidance.

    a. 19285, 19125
    c. 19287
    b. 19125
    d. 19085

12 OPERATIVE PROCEDURE: Excision of back lesion. INDICA-

TIONS FOR SURGERY: The patient has an enlarging lesion on the upper midback. FINDINGS AT SURGERY: There was a 5-cm, upper midback lesion.

OPERATIVE PROCEDURE: With the patient prone, the back was prepped and draped in the usual sterile fashion. The skin and underlying tissues were anesthetized with 30 mL of 1% lidocaine with epinephrine.

Through a 5-cm transverse skin incision, the lesion was excised. Hemostasis was ensured.The incision was closed using 3-0 Vicryl for the deep layers and running 3-0 Prolene subcuticular stitch with Steri-Strips for the skin.

The patient was returned to the same-day surgery center in stable postoperative condition. Allsponge, needle, and instrument counts were correct. Estimated blood loss is 0 mL. PATHOLOGY REPORT LATER INDICATED: Follicular cyst, infundibular type, skin of back.

    a. 11406, 12002   c. 11406, 12032
    b. 11424   d. 11606

13. What code(s) would be used to code a split-thickness skin graft, both thighs to the abdomen, measuring 45 x 21 cm?
    a. 15100, 15101 x 9
    b. 15100, 15101
    c. 15110, 15111
    d. 15100, 15111

Musculoskeletal System

14. Carl Ostrick, a 21-year-old male, slipped on a patch of ice on his sidewalk while shoveling snow. When he fell, his left hand was wedged under his body and his carpometacarpal joint was dislocated. After manipulating the joint back into normal alignment, the surgeon fixed the dislocation by placing a wire percutaneously through the carpometacarpal joint to maintain alignment.
    a. 26608-F1   c. 26706-LT
    b. 26650-FA   d. 26676-LT

15. Mary tells her physician that she has been having pain in her left wrist for several weeks. The physician examines the area and palpates a ganglion cyst of the tendon sheath. He marks the injection sites, sterilizes the area, and injects corticosteroid into two areas.
    a. 20550-LT x 2, M67.432   c. 20551-LT x 2, M67.40
    b. 20551-LT, M67.432   d. 20612-LT, 20612-59-LT, M67.432

16. Libby was thrown from a horse while riding in the ditch; a truck that honked the horn as it passed her startled her horse. The horse reared up, and Libby was thrown to the ground. Her left tibia was fractured and required insertion of multiple pins to stabilize the defect area. A unilateral multiplane external fixation system was then attached to the pins. Code the placement of the fixation device and diagnosis only.

a. 20661-LT, S82.202A, V88.9XXA
b. 20692-LT, S82.201A, V80.11XA
c. 20692-LT, S82.202A, V80.010A
d. 20690-LT, S82.201A, V80.11XA

17 John, an 84-year-old male, tripped while on his morning walk. He stated he was thinking about something else when he inadvertently tripped over the sidewalk curb and fell to his knees. X-ray indicated a fracture of his right patella. With the patient under general anesthesia, the area was opened and extensively irrigated. The left aspect of the patella was severely fragmented, and a portion of the patella was subsequently removed. The remaining patella fractures were wired. The surrounding tissue was repaired, thoroughly irrigated, and closed in the usual manner.
a. 27524-RT, S82.001A, W10.1XXA
b. 27520-RT, S82.001A, W10.1XXA
c. 27524-RT, S82.009C, W19.XXXA
d. 27524-RT, S82.001A, W19.XXXA

18 Darin was a passenger in an automobile rollover accident and was not wearing a seat belt at the time. He was thrown from the automobile and was pinned under the rear of the overturned vehicle. He sustained craniofacial separation that required complicated internal and external fixation using an open approach to repair the extensive damage. A halo device was used to hold the head immobile.
a. 21435, 20661   c. 21432
b. 21435   d. 21436, 20661

19 A small incision was made over the left proximal tibia, and a traction pin was inserted through the bone to the opposite side. Weights were then affixed to the pins to stabilize the tibial fracture temporarily until fracture repair could be performed.
a. 20650-LT   c. 20690-LT
b. 20663-LT   d. 20692-LT

Cardio And Respiratory System

20 OPERATIVE PROCEDURE
PREOPERATIVE DIAGNOSIS: 68-year-old male in a coma. POSTOPERATIVE DIAGNOSIS: 68-year-old male in a coma.
PROCEDURE PERFORMED: Placement of a triple lumen central line in right subclavian vein. With the usual Betadine scrub to the right subclavian vein area and with a second attempt, the subclavian vein was cannulated and the wire was threaded. The first time the wire did not thread right, and so the attempt was aborted to make sure we had good identification of structures. Once the wire was in place the needle was removed and a tissue dilator was pushed into position over the wire. Once that was removed, then the central lumen catheter was pushed into position at 17 cm and the wire removed. All three ports were flushed. The catheter was sewn into position, and a dressing applied.
    a. 36011, R40.0   c. 36556, R40.0
    b. 36011, R40.20   d. 36556, R40.20

21
PREOPERATIVE DIAGNOSIS: Atelectasis of the left lower lobe.
PROCEDURE PERFORMED: Fiberoptic bronchoscopy with brushings and cell washings. PROCEDURE: The patient was already sedated, on a ventilator, and intubated; so his bronchoscopy was done through the ET tube. It was passed easily down to the carina. About 2 to 2.5 cm above the carina, we could see the trachea, which appeared good, as was the carina. In the right lung, all segments were patent and entered, and no masses were seen. The left lung, however, had petechial ecchymotic areas scattered throughout the airways. The tissue was friable and swollen, but no mucous plugs were noted, and all the airways were open, just somewhat swollen. No abnor-

mal secretions were noted at all. Brushings were taken as well as washings, including some with Mucomyst to see whether we could get some distal mucous plug, but nothing really significant was returned. The specimens were sent to appropriate cytological and bacteriological studies. The patient tolerated the procedure fairly well.

    a. 31622, 31623-51   c. 31622-RT, 31623-51-LT
    b. 31623   d. 31624

22 Code only the operative procedure and diagnosis (es). PREOPERATIVE DIAGNOSIS: Hypoxia, Pneumothorax POSTOPERATIVE DIAGNOSIS: Hypoxia, Pneumothorax

PROCEDURE: Chest tube placement

DESCRIPTION OF PROCEDURE: The patient was previously sedated with Versed and paralyzed with Nimbex. Lidocaine was used to numb the incision area in the midlateral left chest at about nipple level. After the lidocaine, an incision was made, and we bluntly dissected to the area of the pleural space, making sure we were superior to the rib. On entrance to the pleural space, there was immediate release of air noted. An 18-gauge chest tube was subsequently placed and sutured to the skin. There were no complications for the procedure, and blood loss was minimal.

DISPOSITION: Follow-up, single-view, chest x-ray showed significant resolution of the pneumothorax except for a small apical pneumothorax that was noted.

    a. 32554   c. 32551
    b. 32550   d. 32505

23 What code would you use to report the percutaneous insertion of a dual- chamberpacemaker by means of the subclavian vein?

    a. 33249   c. 33208
    b. 33217   d. 33240

24 OPERATIVE REPORT: The patient is in for a bone marrow biopsy. The patient was sterilized by standard procedure. Bone marrow core biopsies were obtained from the

leftposterior iliac crest with minimal discomfort. At the end of the procedure, the patient denied discomfort, without evidence of complications.
  a. 20225
  b. 38221
  c. 38230
  d. 38220

25 This 52-year-old male has undergone several attempts at extubation, all of which failed. He also has morbid obesity and significant subcutaneous fat in his neck. The patient is now in for a flap tracheostomy and cervical lipectomy. The cervical lipectomy is necessary for adequate exposure and access to the trachea and also to secure tracheotomy tube placement.
  a. 31610, 15839-51   c. 31610, 15838
  b. 31610   d. 31603, 15839-51

Digestive System

26 Connie 3week old baby was brought to the operating room for a diaphragmatic hernia, and transthoracic repair was performed.
  a. 43325   c. 43327
  b. 39503   d. 39540

27 This 43-year-old female comes in with a peritonsillar abscess. The patient is brought tosame-day surgery and given general anesthetic. On examination of the peritonsillar abscess, an incision was made and fluid was drained. The area was examined again, saline was applied, and then the area was packed with gauze. The patient tolerated the procedure well.
  a. 42825, J36   c. 42826, J36
  b. 42700, J36   d. 42700

28 The physician is using an abdominal approach to perform a proctopexy combined with asigmoid resection:
  a. 45540   c. 45550
  b. 45541   d. 45342

29 The patient was taken to the operating room for a repair of a recurrent strangulatedinguinal hernia.
   a. 49521
   b. 49520
   c. 49492
   d. 49521-78

30 This patient is brought back to the operating room during the postoperative period by thesame physician to repair an esophagogastrostomy leak, transthoracic approach, done 2 days ago. The patient is status post esophagectomy for cancer. Code the procedure.
   a. 43320-78
   b. 43340-78
   c. 43341
   d. 43415-78

31 PROCEDURE: The video therapeutic endoscope was passed without difficulty into the oropharynx. The gastroesophageal junction was seen at 40 cm. Inspection of the esophagus revealed no erythema, ulceration, varices, or other mucosal abnormalities. The stomach was entered and the endoscope advanced to the second duodenum. Inspection of the second duodenum, first duodenum, duodenal bulb, and pylorus revealed no abnormalities. Retroflexion revealed no lesions along the curvature. Inspection of the antrum, body, and fundus of the stomach revealed no abnormalities. The patient tolerated the procedure well.
   a. 45378
   b. 43235
   c. 49320
   d. 43255

Genitourinary System

32 This 32-year-old female presents with an ectopic pregnancy. The physician performs alaparoscopic salpingectomy.
   a. 59120, O00.9
   b. 59151, O00.9
   c. 58943, O00.1
   d. 59120, O00.8

33 This 41-year-old female presented with a right labial le-

sion. A biopsy was taken, and the results were reported as VIN-III, cannot rule out invasion. The decision was therefore made to proceed with wide local excision of the right vulva.

PROCEDURE: The patient was taken to the operating room, and general anesthesia was administered. The patient was then prepped and draped in the usual manner in lithotomy position, and the bladder was emptied with a straight catheter. The vulva was then inspected. On the right labium minora at approximately the 11 o'clock position, there was

a multifocal lesion. A marking pen was then used to mark out an elliptical incision, leaving a 1-cm border on all sides. The skin ellipse was then excised using a knife. Bleeders were cauterized with electrocautery. A running locked suture of 2-0 Vicryl was then placed in the deeper tissue. The skin was finally reapproximated with 4-0 Vicryl in an interrupted fashion. Good hemostasis was thereby achieved. The patient tolerated this procedure well. There were no complications.

   a. 56605   b. 56625
   c. 56620   d. 11620

34 OPERATIVE REPORT

PREOPERATIVE DIAGNOSIS: Missed abortion with fetal demise, 11 weeks. POSTOPERATIVE DIAGNOSIS: Missed abortion with fetal demise, 11 weeks. PROCEDURE: Suction D&C.

The patient was prepped and draped in a lithotomy position under general mask anesthesia, and the bladder was straight catheterized; a weighted speculum was placed in the vagina. The anterior lip of the cervix was grasped with a single-tooth tenaculum. The uterus was then sounded to a depth of 8 cm. The cervical os was then serially dilated to allow passage of a size 10 curved suction curette. A size 10 curved suction curette was then used to evacuate the intrauterine contents. Sharp curette was used to gently palpate the uterine wall with negative return of tissue, and the suction curette was again used with negative return of tissue. The tenaculum was removed from the cervix. The speculum was removed from the vagina. All sponges and needles were accounted for at completion of

the procedure. The patient left the operating room in apparent good condition having tolerated the procedure well.
a. 59812, O03.9   c. 59820, O02.1
  b. 59812, O07.4   d. 59856, O02.1

35 This 1-year-old boy has a midshaft hypospadias with a very mild degree of chordee. He also has a persistent right hydrocele. The surgeon brought the boy to surgery to perform aright hydrocele repair and one-stage repair of hypospadias with preputialonlay flap.
  a. 54322, 55040   c. 54324, 55060-51
  b. 54322, 55041-51   d. 54324, 55060

36 The pediatric physician takes this newborn male to the nursery to perform a clampcircumcision.
  a. 54160, Z41.2   c. 54150, Z41.2
  b. 54160-52, Z41.2   d. 54150-52, Z41.2

37 This gentleman has worsening bilateral hydronephrosis. He did not have much of a postvoid residual on bladder scan. He is taken to the operating room to have a bilateral cystoscopy and retrograde pyelogram. The results come back as gross prostatic hyperplasia.
  a. 52005, N40.0   c. 52005-50, N40.0, N13.30
  b. 52000, N40.0   d. 52000-50, N13.3

38 This patient is 35 years old at 35 weeks' gestation. She presented in spontaneous labor. Because of her prior cesarean section, she is taken to the operating room to have a repeatlower-segment transverse cesarean section performed. The patient also desires sterilization, and so a bilateral tubal ligation will also be performed. A single liveborn infant was the outcome of the delivery.
a. 59510, 58600-51, Z30.2
b. 59620, 58611, O60.14X0, Z37.0, Z30.2
c. 59514, 58605-51, Z37.0, O60.14X0

d. 59514, 58611, O60.14X0, O34.21, Z37.0, Z30.2

Nervous, Eye, Ear And Thyroid

39 What code would you assign to report a left partial thyroid lobectomy, withisthmusectomy?
    a. 60210   c. 60212
    b. 60220   d. 60225

40 This patient came in with an obstructed ventriculoperitoneal shunt. The procedure performed was to be a revision of shunt. After inspecting the shunt system, the entire cerebrospinal fluid shunt system was removed and a similar replacement shunt systemwas placed.
    a. 62180   c. 62256
    b. 62258   d. 62190

41 OPERATIVE REPORT
PREOPERATIVE DIAGNOSIS: Fever.
PROCEDURE PERFORMED: Lumbar puncture.
DESCRIPTION OF PROCEDURE: The patient was placed in the lateral decubitus position with the left side up. The legs and hips were flexed into the fetal position The lumbosacral area was sterilely prepped. It was then numbed with 1% Xylocaine. I then placed a 22-gauge spinal needle on the first pass into the intrathecal space between the L4 and L5 spinous processes. The fluid was minimally xanthochromic. I sent the fluid for cell count for differential, protein, glucose, Gram stain, and culture. The patient tolerated the procedure well without apparent complication. The needle was removed at the end of the procedure. The area was cleansed, and a Band-Aid was placed.
    a. 62272   c. 62272, 62270

b. 62268   d. 62270

42 This 66-year-old male has been diagnosed with a senile cataract of the posterior subcapsular and is scheduled for a cataract extraction by phacoemulsification of the righteye. The physician has taken the patient to the operating room to perform a posterior subcapsular cataract extraction with IOL, diffuse of the right eye.
   a. 66982-RT   c. 66983-RT
   b. 66984-RT   d. 66830-RT

43 Marginal laceration involving the left lower eyelid and laceration of the left upper eyelidinvolving the tarsus. Both required full-thickness repair. Also there were multiple
stellate lacerations above the left eye, totaling 24.2 cm and requiring full-thickness layered repair.
   a. 67935-E2, 12017
   b. 67930-E2, 13152-51, 13153
   c. 67935-E2, 67935-E1-51, 12056-51
   d. 67935-E2, 12017-51

44 Left frontal ventricular puncture for implanting catheter, layered repair of 8-cm scalp laceration, and repair of multiple facial and eyelid lacerations with an approximate totallength of 12 cm.
   a. 61020, 12015-51   c. 61215, 12015-51
   b. 61107, 12034-51, 12015-51   d. 61107, 12034-51

E/M

45 Sam, a 4-year-old male, was brought to the emergency department by his mother, whereDr. Black, the emergency department physician, examined the child. Dr. Black has not provided service to this child in the past. During a problem-focused history, the mother stated that the child has had a temperature of 101º F for the

past 24 hours, has been veryfussy, and has been pulling on his left ear. The physician examined the child during a problem-focused examination and diagnosed otitis media, for which he prescribed a 10day course of amoxicillin.

a. 99202
b. 99212
c. 99241
d. 99281

46 Bill, a retired U.S. Air Force pilot, was on observation status 12 hours to assess the outcome of a fall from the back of a pickup truck into a gravel pit. The physician discharged Bill from observation that same day after determining that no further monitoring of his condition was necessary. The physician provided a comprehensivehistory and examination and indicated that the medical decision making was of a lowcomplexity.

a. 99218, Z04.9, W18.30XA, W18.30XA
b. 99234, Z04.3, W17.89XA, Z04.3, W18.30XA
c. 99217, Z04.3, W18.30XA
d. 99234, 99217,

47 A neurological consultation in the emergency department of the local hospital is requested for a 25-year-old male with suspected closed head trauma. The patient had a loss of consciousness (LOC) this morning after receiving a blow to the head in a high school basketball game. He presents to the emergency department with a headache, dizziness, and confusion. During the comprehensive history, the girlfriend relates that the patient has been very irritable and confused since the incident.

Physical examination reveals the patient to be unsteady and exhibiting difficulty in concentration when statingmonths in reverse. The pupils dilate unequally. The physician continues with a comprehensive examination involving an extensive review of neurological function. Theneurologist orders a stat CT and MRI. The physician suspects a subdural hematoma or an epidural hematoma,

and the medical decision making complexity is high.
 a. 99285
 b. 99253
 c. 99245
 d. 99255

48 Karra Hendricks, a 37-year-old female, is an established patient who presents to the office with pain in the RLQ with fever. The physician takes a detailed history and performs a detailed examination. The medical decision making is noted to be of a low complexity.
 a. 99203
 b. 99213
 c. 99214
 d. 99221

49 A 57-year-old male was sent by his family physician to a urologist for an office consultation. The patient has had bright red blood in his urine sporadically for the past 3 weeks. The urologist obtains a detailed history from the patient and continues with a detailed physical examination. The urologist recommends a cystoscopy to be scheduled for the following week and discusses the procedure and risks with the patient. The medical decision making is of moderate complexity. Report only the office service.
 a. 99243-57
 b. 99244-57, 52000
 c. 99253
 d. 99221

50 An obstetrician is requested to provide an office consultation to a 23-year-old female with first-trimester bleeding. The patient presents with a history of brownish discharge and occasional pinkish discharge. During the comprehensive history, the patient relates that she has had suprapubic pain in the past week and cramping. She has felt nausea and has vomited on three occasions. On one occasion, the nausea was accompanied by dizziness and vertigo. The physician conducts a comprehensive examination focused on the patient's chief complaint. The uterus is found to be soft and involuted. There is cervical motion tenderness and significant abdominal tenderness on palpation. A left pelvic mass is palpated in the left quadrant. The physician orders a

pelvic ultrasound, a complete CBC, and differential. Considering the range of possible diagnoses, the medical decision-making complexity is high.

a. 99255

b. 99242

c. 99245

d. 99235

Anesthesia

51 What code describes the anesthesia for closed chest procedure including bronchoscopy

a. 00520
b. 00528
c. 00560
d. 00540

52 The following is the anesthesia formula: a.

BTC
b. TBC
c. BTQ
d. BTM

53 Which HCPCS modifier indicates an anesthesia service in which the anesthesiologist medically directs one CRNA?

a. QX
b. QY
c. QZ
d. QK

Radiology

54 This 69-year-old female is in for a magnetic resonance examination of the brain because of new seizure activity. After imaging without contrast, contrast was administered and further sequences were performed. Examination results indicated no apparent neoplasm or vascular malformation.

a. 70543-26, 70553   c. 70559
b. 70543-26   d. 70553

55 This patient is suffering from primary lung cancer and is in for a follow-up CT scan of the thorax with contrast material. Code the physician component only.
   a. 71250-26   c. 71260-26
   b. 71260   d. 71270-26

56 EXAMINATION OF:
   Abdomen and pelvis. CLINICAL SYMPTOMS:
   Ascites.
CT OF ABDOMEN AND PELVIS: Technique: CT of the abdomen and pelvis was performed without oral or IV contrast material per physician request. No previous CT scans for comparison.
FINDINGS: No ascites. Moderate-sized pleural effusion on the right.
   a. 74150-26   c. 74176
   b. 74176-26   d. 74150

57 EXAMINATION OF:
   Cervical spine. CLINICAL SYMPTOMS:

Herniated disk.

FINDINGS: A single spot fluoroscopic film from the operating room is submitted for interpretation. The cervical spine is not well demonstrated above the level of the inferior aspect of C6. There is a metallic surgical plate seen anterior to the cervical spine. The cephalic portion of the plate is at the level of C6 at its superior endplate. That extends in an inferior direction, presumably anterior to C7; however, there is not adequate visualization of C7 to confirm location. Density overlies the C6-7 intervertebral disk space, suggesting the presence of a bone plug in this area; however, again visualization is not adequate in this area. Further evaluation with plain radiographs is recommended.

    a. 72100-26   b. 72020-26
    c. 72100-52-26   d. 72020-52-26

58 This patient undergoes a gallbladder sonogram due to epigastric pain. The report indicatesthat the visualized portions of the liver are normal. No free fluid noted within Morison's pouch. The gallbladder is identified and is empty. No evidence of wall thickening or surrounding fluid is seen. There is no ductal dilatation. The common hepatic duct and common bile duct measure 0.4 and 0.8 cm, respectively. The common bile duct measurement is at the upper limits of normal.

    a. 76700-26   c. 76775-26
    b. 76705-26   d. 76705

59 EXAMINATION OF: Chest. CLINICAL SYMPTOMS: Pneumonia.PA AND LATERAL CHEST X-RAY

CONCLUSION: Ventilation within the lung fields has improved compared with previous study.

a. 71046-26, J15.8   c. 71046-26, J18.9
b. 71048, J15.6   d. 71046, J18.9

Lab And Path

60 Code a pregnancy test, urine.
   a. 84702   c. 81025
   b. 84703   d. 84702 X 2

61 This patient is in for a kidney biopsy (50200) because a mass was identified by ultrasound. The specimen is sent to pathology for gross and microscopic examination. Report the technical and professional components for this service. The results were inconclusive.
   a. 88305-26   c. 88307
   b. 88307-26   d. 88305

62 This patient presented to the laboratory yesterday for a creatine measurement. The resultscame back at higher than normal levels; therefore, the patient was asked to return to the laboratory today for a repeat creatine test before the nephrologist is consulted. Report thesecond day of test only.
   a. 82540 X 2   c. 82550
   b. 82550x2   d. 82540

63 This 69-year-old female presents to the laboratory after her physician ordered troponin, quantitative, and troponin, qualitative assay, to assist in the diagnosis of her chief complaint of acute onset of chest pain.
   a. 84484, 80299, R07.2   c. 84484, 84512, R07.9
   b. 84512, 84484, 80299, R07.89   d. 84484, 84512, R07.89

64 This is a patient with atrial fibrillation who comes

to the clinic laboratory routinely for aquantitative digoxin level.
a. 80305, I48.2
b. 80306, I48.91
c. 80162, I48.91
d. 80162, I48.0

65 What code would you use to code a bilirubin, total (transcutaneous)?

a. 82247
b. 88399
c. 88740
d. 88720

Medicine

66 This 40-year-old patient who is a type 2 diabetic is seen in an inpatient setting for psychotherapy. The doctor spends 50 minutes face to face with the patient. The patient isseen for depression.
a. 90834, F32.9, E11.8
b. 90837, F32.9, E11.8
c. 90834, F32.9
d. 90837, F32.9

67 A patient presents for a pleural cavity chemotherapy session with 10 mg doxorubicin HClthat requires a thoracentesis to be performed:
a. 96446, J9000
b. 96440, 32554, J9000
c. 96440, J9000
d. 96446, 32555, J9000

68 Which code would be used to report an EEG (electroencephalogram) provided duringcarotid surgery?
a. 95816
b. 95819
c. 95822
d. 95955

69 Which code would be used to report an EEG (electroencephalogram) provided duringcarotid surgery?

a. 95816 c. 95822
b. 95819 d. 95955

70 DIALYSIS INPATIENT NOTE: This 24-year-old male patient is on continuous ambulatory peritoneal dialysis (CAPD) using 1.5%. He drains more than 600 mL. He is tolerating dialysis well. He continues to have some abdominal pain, but his abdomen is not distended. He has some diarrhea. His abdomen does not look like acute abdomen. His vitals, other than blood pressure in the 190s over 100s, are fine. He is afebrile. At this time, I will continue with 1.5% dialysate. I gave him labetalol IV for blood pressure. Because of diarrhea, I am going to check stool for white cells, culture. Next we will see what the primary physician says today. His HIDA scan was normal. The patient suffers from ESRD.

a. 90947, 90935, N18.6, N19.7   c. 90947, N18.6
b. 90945, N18.6, N19.7   d. 90945, N18.6

71 What code would be used to code the technical aspect of an evaluation of swallowing by video recording using a flexible fiberoptic endoscope?

a. 92611   c. 92610
b. 92612   d. 92613

Anatomy And Terminology

72 Which of the following terms means taste?
a. Meissner
b. pacinian
c. gustatory

d. astrocytes c

73 This suffix means to act upon:
   a. -in   c. -tropin
   b. -ine   d. -agon

74 Which of the following terms does NOT describe a receptor of the body?
   a. mechanoreceptor
   b. proprioceptor
   c. thermoreceptor
   d. endoreceptor

75 This is the first portion of the small intestine:
   a. jejunum   b. ileum
   c. dudenum   d. cecum

76 The middle layer of the skin, also known as the corium or true skin, is the:

   a. Epidermis.   c. Dermis.
   b. Stratum corneum.   d. subcutaneous

77 This term means the use of electric current to destroy tissue: a..eventration   c. evisceration
   b. enterolysis   d. fulguration

78 This is the collarbone:
   A, patella   c. scapula
   b, tibia   d. clavicle

79 The act of turning upward, such as the hand turned palm upward:

a. supination   c. pronation
b. adduction   d. circumduction

Icd 10 Cm

80 Open wound of left hand
   A, S61.402A   C. S48.019A
   B, S61.209A   D, S48.029A

81 Admission for hemodialysis and acute renal failure

   A. Z49.31, N17.8
   B Z49.01, N17.8
   C. Z49.31, N17.9
   D. N17.9, Z49.31

82 Four-week-old female with obstructive apnea

   A P28.3   c. P28.2
   b. P28.4   d. P28.5

83. Fracture of the right patella with abrasion.
   a. S82.001D, S80.211A   c. S82.001A, S80.211A
   b. S82.001A   d. S82.001D

84 Congenital hypothyroidism with mild retardation.
a. E03.1, F70   c. E03.1, F71
b. E03.8, F70   d. E03.8, F71

Hcpcs

85 A patient is issued a 22-inch seat cushion for his wheelchair.
a. E0995   c. E0190
b. E0950   d. E2601

86 A patient with chronic lumbar pain previously purchased a TENS and now needs replacement batteries.
a. E1592   c. A4772
b. A5082   d. A4630

87 A patient with chronic obstructive pulmonary disease is issued a medically necessary nebulizer with a compressor and humidifier for extensive use with oxygen delivery.
a. E0570, E0550   c. E0580, E0550

b. E0555, E0570　　　　　　d. E0575, E0550

Complaints And Regulatory

88 Which part of medicare cover the inpatient stay
   A, part A   b. part b
   c. both a and b   c. part d

89 An ABN must be sign, when?

   A, once the insurance company has denigned payment b.. before the service or procedure provided to patient
   c. after services are renderd
   d. once the denied claim has been appeared at the highest level

90 which part of the medicare cover the office services
   a, Part A   b. part b
   c. part A and B   d, part D

Case Study

91 EMERGENCY DEPARTMENT
   REPORT CHIEF COMPLAINT:
   Nasal bridge laceration.
   SUBJECTIVE: The patient is a 74-year-old male who presents to the emergency department with a laceration to the bridge of his nose. He fell in the bathroom tonight. He recalls the incident. He just sort of lost his balance. He denies any vertigo. He denies any chest pain or shortness of breath. He denies any head pain or neck pain. There was no loss of consciousness. He slipped on a wet floor in the bathroom and lost his balance; that is how it happened. He has not had any blood from the nose or mouth.

PAST MEDICAL HISTORY: Parkinson's, Back pain, Constipation MEDICATIONS: See the patient record for a complete list of medications.

ALLERGIES: NA.

REVIEW OF SYSTEMS: Per HPI. Otherwise, negative.

PHYSICAL EXAMINATION: The exam showed a 74-year-old male in no acute distress. Examination of the HEAD showed no obvious trauma other than the bridge of the nose, where there is approximately a 1.5- to 2-cm laceration. He had no bony tenderness under this. Pupils were equal, round, and reactive. EARS and NOSE: OROPHARYNX was unremarkable. NECK was soft and supple. HEART was regular. LUNGS were clear but slightly diminished in the bases.

PROCEDURE: The wound was draped in a sterile fashion and anesthetized with 1% Xylocaine with sodium bicarbonate. It was cleansed with sterile saline and then repaired using interrupted 6-0 Ethilon sutures (Dr. Barney Teller, first-year resident, assisted with the suturing).

ASSESSMENT: Nasal bridge laceration, status post fall.

Plan: Keep clean. Sutures out in 5 to 7 days. Watch for signs of infection.

a. 12051, S01.21XA, W18.49XA

b. 12011, S01.21XA, W18.49XA

c 12011, S01.20XA, W18.49XA

d. 12011, 11000, S01.20XA, W18.49XA

92 OPERATIVE REPORT
PREOPERATIVE DIAGNOSIS: Leaking from intestinal anastomosis. POSTOPERATIVE DIAGNOSIS: Leaking from intestinal anastomosis. PROCEDURE PERFORMED: Proximal ileostomy for diversion of colon. Oversew of right colonic fistula.
OPERATIVE NOTE: This patient was taken back to the operating room from the intensive care unit. She was having acute signs of leakage from an anastomosis I performed 3 days previously. We took down some of the sutures holding the wound together. We basically exposed all of this patient's intestine. It was evident that she was leaking from the small bowel as well as from the right colon. I thought the only thing we could do would be to repair the right colon. This was done in two layers, and then we freed up enough bowel to try to make an ileostomy proximal to the area of leakage. We were able to do this with great difficulty, and there was only a small amount of bowel to be brought out. We brought this out as an ileostomy stoma, realizing that it was of questionable viability and that it should be watched closely. With that accomplished, we then packed the wound and returned the patient to the intensive care unit.
   a. 44310   c. 45136
   b. 44310-78   d. 45136-78

93 OPERATIVE REPORT
PREOPERATIVE DIAGNOSIS: Possible recurrent transitional cell carcinoma of the bladder.
POSTOPERATIVE DIAGNOSIS: No evidence of recurrence. PROCEDURE PERFORMED: Cystoscopy with multiple bladder biopsies.
PROCEDURE NOTE: The patient was given a general mask anesthetic, prepped, and draped in the lithotomy position. The 21-French cystoscope was passed into the bladder. There was a hyperemic area on the posterior wall of the bladder, and a biopsy was taken. Random biopsies of the bladder were also performed. This area was fulgurated. A

total of 7 sq cm of bladder was fulgurated. A catheter was left at the end of the procedure. The patient tolerated the procedure well and was transferred to the recovery room in good condition. The pathology report indicated no evidence of recurrence.

    a. 52224
    b. 51020, 52204
    c. 52234
    d. 52224 X 4

94 OPERATIVE REPORT

PREOPERATIVE DIAGNOSIS: Right ureteral stricture. POSTOPERATIVE DIAGNOSIS: Right ureteral stricture. PROCEDURE PERFORMED: Cystoscopy, right ureteral stent change.

PROCEDURE NOTE: The patient was placed in the lithotomy position after receiving IV sedation. He was prepped and draped in the lithotomy position. The 21-French cystoscope was passed into the bladder, and urine was collected for culture Inspection of the bladder demonstrated findings consistent with radiation cystitis, which has been previously diagnosed. There is no frank neoplasia. The right ureteral stent was grasped and removed through the urethral meatus; under fluoroscopic control, a guide wire was advanced up the stent, and the stent was exchanged for a 7-French 26-cm stent under fluoroscopic control in the usual fashion. The patient tolerated the procedure well.

    a. 51702-LT, N13.5
    b. 52005-RT, N30.90
    c. 52332-RT, N30.90
    d. 52332-RT, N13.5

95 OPERATIVE REPORT

PREOPERATIVE DIAGNOSIS: Herniated disk L4-5 on the left.
PROCEDURE PERFORMED: Laminotomy, foraminotomy, removal of herniated disk L4-5 on the left.
PROCEDURE: Under general anesthesia, the patient was placed in the prone position and the back was prepped and draped in the usual manner. An incision was made in the skin extending through subcutaneous tissue. Lumbodorsal fascia was divided. The erector spinae muscles were bluntly dissected from

the lamina of L4-5 on the left. The interspace was localized. I then performed a generous laminotomy and foraminotomy here, and retracted on the nerve root. It was obvious there was a herniated disk. I removed it, entered the space, and removed degenerating material, satisfied that I had decompressed the root well. There were free fragments lying around beneath the nerve root. We removed all of these. I was able to pass a hockey stick down the foramen across the midline, satisfied I had taken out the large fragments from the interspace at L4-5, and decompressed it well. I irrigated the wound well, put a Hemovac drain in the wound, and then closed the wound in layers using doubleknotted 0 chromic on the lumbodorsal fascia with Vicryl, 2-0 plain in the subcutaneous tissue and surgical staples on the skin. A dressing was applied. The patient was discharged to the recovery room.

a. 63030-LT
b. 63012-LT
c. 63047-LT
d. 63047-LT, 63048-LT

96 OPERATIVE REPORT
PREOPERATIVE DIAGNOSIS: Brain tumor versus abscess. PROCEDURE: Craniotomy.
DESCRIPTION OF PROCEDURE: Under general anesthesia, the patient's head was prepped and draped in the usual manner. It was placed in Mayfield pins. We then proceeded with a craniotomy. An inverted U-shaped incision was made over the posterior right occipital area. The flap was turned down. Three burr holes were made. Having done this, I then localized the tumor through the burr holes and dura. We then made an incision in the dura in an inverted
U-shaped fashion. The cortex looked a little swollen but normal. We then used the localizer to locate the cavity. I separated the gyrus and got right into the cavity and saw pus, which was removed. Cultures were taken and sent for pathology report, which came back later describing the presence of clusters of gram-positive cocci, confirming that this was an abscess. We cleaned out the abscessed cavity using irrigation and suction. The bed of the abscessed cavity was cauterized. Then a small piece of Gelfoam was used for hemostasis.
Satisfied that it was dry, I closed the dura. I approximated the

scalp. A dressing was applied. The patient was discharged to the recovery room.
- a. 61154, G06.0
- b. 61154, D49.6
- c. 61320, G06.0
- d. 61150, D49.6

97 This patient is a 52-year-old female who has been having prolonged and heavy bleeding. SURGICAL FINDINGS: On pelvic exam under anesthesia, the uterus was normal size and firm. The examination revealed no masses. She had a few small endometrial polyps in the lower uterine segment.
DESCRIPTION OF PROCEDURE: After induction of general anesthesia, the patient was placed in the dorsolithotomy position, after which the perineum and vagina were prepped, the bladder straight catheterized, and the patient draped. After bimanualexam was performed, a weighted speculum was placed in the vagina and the anterior lip of the cervix was grasped with a single toothed tenaculum. An endocervical curettage was then done with a Kevorkian curet. The uterus was then sounded to 8.5 cm. The endocervical canal was dilated to 7 mm with Hegar dilators. A 5.5-mm Olympus hysteroscope was introduced using a distention medium. The cavity was systematically inspected, and the preceding findings noted The hysteroscope was withdrawn and the cervix further dilated to 10 mm. Polyp forceps was introduced, and a few small polyps were removed. These were sent separately. Sharp endometrial curettage was then done. The hysteroscope was then reinserted, and the polyps had essentially been removed. The patient tolerated the procedure well and returned to the recovery room in stable condition. Pathology confirmed benign endometrial polyps.

    a. 58558, 57460-51, N92.0, N84.0
    b. 58558, N92.0, N84.0
    c. 58558, 57558-51, N92.0, N84.0
    d. 58558, N92.1, D49.

98 OPERATIVE REPORT
PREOPERATIVE DIAGNOSIS: Open fracture, left humerus, with possible loss of left radial pulse.
PROCEDURE PERFORMED: Open reduction internal fixation, left open humerus fracture. PROCEDURE: While under a general anesthetic, the patient's left arm was

prepped with Betadine and draped in sterile fashion. We then created a longitudinal incision over the anterolateral aspect of his left arm and carried the dissection through the subcutaneous tissue. We attempted to identify the lateral intermuscular septum and progressed to the fracture site, which was actually fairly easy to do because there was some significant tearing and rupturing of the biceps and brachialis muscles. These were partial ruptures, but the bone was relatively easy to expose through this. We then identified the fracture site and thoroughly irrigated it with several liters of saline. We also noted that the radial nerve was easily visible, crossing along the posterolateral aspect of the fracture site. It was intact. We carefully etected it throughout the remainder of the procedure. We then were able to strip the periosteum away from the lateral side of the shaft of the humerus both proximally and distally from the fracture site. We did this just enough to apply a 6-hole plate, which we eventually held in place with six cortical screws. We did attempt to compress the fracture site. Due to some comminution, the fracture was not quite anatomically aligned, but certainly it was felt to be very acceptable. Once we had applied the plate, we then checked the radial pulse with a Doppler. We found that the radial pulse was present using the Doppler, but not with palpation. We then applied Xeroform dressings to the wounds and the incision. After padding the arm thoroughly, we applied a long-arm splint with the elbow flexed about 75 degrees. He tolerated the procedure well, and the radial pulse was again present on Doppler examination at the end of the procedure.

      a. 24515-RT   c. 24515-LT
      b. 24500-LT   d. 24505-LT

99 OPERATIVE REPORT

PREOPERATIVE DIAGNOSIS: Left thigh abscess.
PROCEDURE PERFORMED: Incision and drainage of left thigh abscess. OPERATIVE NOTE: With the patient under general anesthesia, he was placed in the lithotomy position. The area around the anus was carefully inspected, and we saw no evidence of communication with the perirectal space. This appears to have risen in

the crease at the top of the leg, extending from the posterior buttocks region up toward the side of the base of the penis. In any event, the area was prepped and draped in a sterile manner. Then we incised the area in fluctuation. We obtained a lot of very foul-smelling, almost stool-like material (it was not stool, but it was brown and very foul-smelling material). This was not the typical pus one sees with a Staphylococcus aureus-type infection. The incision was widened to allow us to probe the cavity fully. Again, I could see no evidence of communication to the rectum, but there was extension down the thigh and extension up into the groin crease. The fascia was darkened from the purulent material. I opened some of the fascia to make sure the underlying muscle was viable. This appeared viable. No gas was present. There was nothing to suggest a necrotizing fasciitis. The patient did have a very extensive inflammation within this abscess cavity. The abscess cavity was irrigated with peroxide and saline and packed with gauze vaginal packing. The patient tolerated the procedure well and was discharged from the operating room in stable condition.

a. 26990-LT, L03.119
b. 27301-LT, L02.416
c. 27301-LT, L02.412
d. 27025-LT, L03.416

100 OPERATIVE REPORT
PREOPERATIVE DIAGNOSIS: Atherosclerotic heart disease. POSTOPERATIVE DIAGNOSIS: Atherosclerotic heart disease.
OPERATIVE PROCEDURE: Coronary bypass grafts 2 with a single graft from the aorta to the distal left anterior descending and from the aorta to the distal right coronary artery.
PROCEDURE: The patient was brought to the operating room and placed in a supine position. Under general intubation anesthesia, the anterior chest and legs were prepped and draped in the usual manner. A segment of greater saphenous vein was harvested from the left thigh,

utilizing the endoscopic vein harvesting technique, and prepared for grafting. The sternum was opened in the usual fashion, and the left internal mammary artery was taken down and prepared for grafting. The flow through the internal mammary artery was very poor. The patient did have a 25-mm difference in arterial pressure between the right and left arms, the right arm being higher. The left internal mammary artery was therefore not used.

The pericardium was incised sharply and a pericardial well created. The patient was systemically heparinized and placed on bicaval to aortic cardiopulmonary bypass with the sump in the main pulmonary artery for cardiac decompression. The patient was cooled to 26°C, and on fibrillation an aortic cross-clamp was applied and potassium-rich cold crystalline cardioplegic solution was administered through the aortic root with satisfactory cardiac arrest. Subsequent doses were given down the vein grafts as the anastomoses were completed and via the coronary sinus in a retrograde fashion. Attention was directed to the right coronary artery. The end of the greater saphenous vein was then anastomosed thereto with 7-0 continuous Prolene distally. The remaining graft material was then grafted to the left anterior descending at the junction of the middle and distal third. The aortic cross-clamp was removed after 149 minutes with spontaneous cardioversion. The usual maneuvers to remove air from the left heart were then carried out using transesophageal echocardiographic technique. After all the air was removed and the patient had returned to a satisfactory temperature, he was weaned from cardiopulmonary bypass after 213 minutes utilizing 5 g per kilogram per minute of dopamine. The chest was closed in the usual fashion. A sterile compression dressing was applied, and the patient returned to the surgical intensive care unit in satisfactory condition.

    a. 33511, 33517, I25.110
    b. 33511, 33508, I25.10
    c. 33534, 33508, I25.110
    d. 33511, 33517, I25.10

Exam - 6

1. This term means the surgical removal of the fallopian tube:
    A. ligation
    B. hysterectomy
    C. salpingostomy
    D. salpingectomy

2. This combining form means thirst:
    A. dips/o
    B. acr/o
    C. cortic/o
    D. somat/o

3. This term is also known as a homograft:
    A. autograft
    B. allograft
    C. xenograft
    D. zenograft

4. Which of the following terms does NOT describe a receptor of the body?
    A. mechanoreceptor
    B. proprioceptor
    C. thermoreceptor
    D. endoreceptor

5. This is the first portion of the small intestine:
    A. Jejunum
    B. Ileum
    C. Duodenum
    D. cecum

CPC EXAM PRACTICE 2022

6. This is a part of the inner ear:
   A. vestibule
   B. malleus
   C. incus
   D. stapes

7. This is the area behind the cornea:
   A. anterior chamber
   B. choroid layer
   C. ciliary body
   D. fundus

8. This is the collarbone:
   A. patella
   B. tibia
   C. scapula
   D. clavicle

9. Admission for hemodialysis because of acute renal failure. A. N17.8, Z91.15
   B. N17.0, Z49.01
   C. N17.9, Z99.2
   D. N19, Z49.0

10. Sarcoidosis with cardiomy-opathy. A.

D86.85
B. D86.87
C. I43, D86.9
D. D86.9, I42.9

11. Laceration of left hand.
    A. S61.402A
    B. S61.412A
    C. S61.412D
    D. S61.422A

12. Fracture of the right patella with abrasion.
    A. S02.80XA
    B. S82.001A
    C. S82.009A
    D. S82.001D

13. Mr. Hallberger is 62 and has multiple problems. I am examining him in the intensive critical care unit. I understand he has fluid overload with acute renal failure and was started on ultrafiltration by the nephrologist on duty. He has an abnormal chest x-ray. He has preexisting type II diabetes mellitus and sepsis. We are left with a patient now who is still sedated and on a ventilator because of respiratory failure. Code the diagnoses only.

    A. A41.9, R65.20, N17.9, J96.90, E11.9
    B. E87.70, A41.9, R65.20, N17.9, J96.90, E11.9
    C. A41.9, N17.9, J96.90, R93.89, E11.9
    D. A41.9, R65.20, N17.9, J96.90, E11.9, R93.89

14. A patient is issued a 22-inch seat cushion for his wheelchair.
    A. E2601
    B. E0950
    C. E0190
    D. E2602

15. A patient with chronic lumbar pain previously purchased a TENS and now needs replacement batteries.
    A. E1592
    B. A5082
    C. A4772
    D. A4630

16. Which HCPCS modifier indicates the great toe of the right foot?
    A. T1
    B. T3
    C. T4
    D. T5

17. This entity develops and publishes an annual plan that outlines the Medicare monitoring program.
    A. MACs   B. FIs
    C. OIG   D. CMS

18. This program was developed by CMS to promote national correct coding methods and to control inappropriate payment of Part B claims and hospital outpatient claims.
    A. NCCI
    B. NFS
    C. HIPAA
    D. MA-PA

19. What is a NPI?
    A. National Payer Incentive
    B. National Provider Identifier
    C. National Provider Index
    D. National Payer Identification

20. This document is a notification in advance of services that Medicare probably will not pay for and the estimated cost to the patient.
    A. Wavier of Liability
    B. Coordination of Benefits

C. Advanced Beneficiary Notice
D. UPIN

21. Specific coding guidelines in the CPT manual are located in:

   A. the index.
   B. the introduction
   C. the beginning of each section.
   D. Appendix A.

22. Which punctuation mark between codes in the index of the CPT manual indicates a range of codes is available?

    A.   period
    B.   comma
    C.   semicolon
    D.   hyphen

23. The term that indicates this is the type of code for which the full code description can be known only if the common part of the code (the description preceding the semicolon) of a preceding entry isreferenced:

    A.   stand-alone
    B.   indented
    C.   independent
    D.   add-on

24. The symbol that indicates an add-on code is:

    A.   #
    B.   *
    C.   +
    D.   0

25. When you see the symbol ►◄ next to a code in the CPT manual, you know that:

A.   the code is a new code.
B.   the code contains new or revised text
C.   code is a modifier -51 exempt code.
D.   FDA approval is pending.

26. Which of the following is most accurately about the designation —(Separate procedure).|| Theprocedure is:

A.   incidental to another procedure
B.   reported if it is the only procedure performed
C.   reported if the procedure is unrelated to a more major procedure performed at the sametime on the same site

D. All of the above

27. OPERATIVE REPORT

OPERATIVE PROCEDURE: Excision of back lesion.

INDICATIONS FOR SURGERY: The patient has an enlarging lesion on the upper midback. FINDINGS AT SURGERY: There was a 5-cm, upper midback lesion.

OPERATIVE PROCEDURE: With the patient prone, the back was prepped and
draped in the usual sterile fashion. The skin and underlying tissues were anesthetized with 30 mL of 1% lidocaine with epinephrine.

Through a 5-cm transverse skin incision, the lesion was excised. Hemostasis was ensured. The incision was closed using 3-0 Vicryl for the deep layers and running 3-0 Prolene subcuticular stitchwith Steri-Strips for the skin.

The patient was returned to the same-day surgery center in stable postoperative condition. All sponge, needle, and instrument counts were correct. Estimated blood loss is 0 mL.

PATHOLOGY REPORT LATER INDICATED: Dermatofibroma, skin of back. Assign code(s) for the physician service only.

A. 11406, 12002, D21.9
B. 11424, D21.1
C. 11406, 12032, D21.6
D. 11606, D21.22

28. EMERGENCY DEPARTMENT REPORT CHIEF COMPLAINT: Nasal bridge laceration. SUBJECTIVE: The patient is a 74-year-old male who presents to the emergency department with a laceration to the bridge of his nose. He fell in the bathroom tonight. He recalls the incident. He just sort of lost his balance. He denies any vertigo. He denies any chest pain or shortness of breath. He denies any head pain or neck pain. There was no loss of consciousness. He slipped on a wet floor in the bathroom and lost his balance; that is how it happened. He has not had any blood from the nose or mouth.

PAST MEDICAL HISTORY:
1. Parkinson's.
2. Back pain.
3. Constipation.

MEDICATIONS: See the patient record for a complete list of medications. ALLERGIES: NKDA.

REVIEW OF SYSTEMS: Per HPI. Otherwise, negative.

PHYSICAL EXAMINATION: The exam showed a 74-year-old male in no acute distress. Examination of the HEAD showed no obvious trauma other than the bridge of the nose, where there is approximately a 1.5- to 2-cm laceration. He had no bony tenderness under this. Pupils were equal, round, and reactive. EARS and NOSE: OROPHARYNX was unremarkable. NECK was soft and supple. HEART was regular. LUNGS were clear but slightly diminished in the bases. PROCEDURE: The wound was draped in a sterile fashion and anesthetized with 1% Xylocaine with sodium bicarbonate. It was cleansed with sterile saline and then repaired using interrupted 6-0 Ethilonsutures (Dr. Barney Teller, first-year resident, assisted with the suturing).

ASSESSMENT: Nasal bridge laceration, status post fall.
PLAN: Keep clean. Sutures out in 5 to 7 days. Watch for signs of infection.
A. 12051, S012.1XA, G20, W01.XXXA, Y92.091
B. 12011, S012.1XA, G20, W01.0XXA, Y92.091
C. 12011, S012.1XA, G20, W18.39XA, Y92.094
D. 12011, S012.1XA, G20, W18.42XA, Y92.091

29. SAME-DAY SURGERY
DIAGNOSIS: Inverted nipple with mammary duct ectasia, left. OPERATION: Excision of mass deep to left nipple.
With the patient under general anesthesia, a circumareolar incision was made with sharp dissection and carried down into the breast tissue. The nipple complex was raised up using a small retractor. Wegently dissected underneath to free up the nipple entirely. Once this was done, we had the nipple fullyunfolded, and there was some evident mammary duct ectasis. An area 3 × 4 cm was excised using electrocautery. Hemostasis was maintained with the electrocautery, and then the breast tissue deep to the nipple was reconstructed using sutures of 3-0 chromic. Subcutaneous tissue was closed using 3-0 chromic, and then the skin was closed using 4-0 Vicryl. Steri-Strips were applied. The patient tolerated the procedure well and was returned to the recovery area in stable condition. At the end of the procedure, all sponges and instruments were accounted for.
A. 19120-RT
B. 11404-LT
C. 19112
D. 19120-LT

30. This patient returns today for palliative care to her feet. Her toenails have become elongated and thickened, and she is unable to trim them on her own. She states that she has had no problems

and no acute signs of any infection or otherwise to her feet. She returns today strictly for trimming of her toenails.

EXAMINATION: Her pedal pulses are palpable bilaterally. The nails are mycotic, 1 through 4 on the left, and 1 through 3 on the right.

ASSESSMENT: Onychomycosis, 1 through 4 on the left and 1 through 3 on the right.

PLAN: Mild debridement of mycotic nails × 7. This patient is to return to the clinic in 3 to 4 months for follow-up palliative care.

A. 11721 × 7, B35.1

B. 99212, 11721, B49

C. 11719, B35.1

D. 11721, B35.1

31. OPERATIVE REPORT

With the patient having had a wire localization performed by radiology, she was taken to the operating room and, under local anesthesia of the left breast, was prepped and draped in a sterile manner. A breast line incision was made through the entry point of the wire, and a core of tissue surrounding the wire (approximately 1 × 2 cm) was removed using electrocautery for hemostasis. The specimen, including the wire, was then submitted to radiology, and the presence of the lesion within the specimen was confirmed. The wound was checked for hemostasis, and this was maintained with electrocautery. The breast tissue was reapproximated using 2-0 and 3-0 chromic. The skin was closed using 4-0 Vicryl in a subcuticular manner. Steri-Strips were applied. The patient tolerated the procedure well and was discharged from the operating room in stable condition. At the end of the procedure, all sponges and instruments were accounted for.

Pathology report later indicated: Benign lesion.

A. 11602-LT, D24.2

B. 11400-LT, D24.9

C. 19125-LT, D24.2

D. 19125-LT, D49.3

32. What CPT and ICD-10-CM codes would be used to code a split-thickness skin graft, both thighs to the abdomen, measuring 45 × 21 cm performed on a patient who has third-degree burns of the abdomen. Documentation stated 20% of the body surface was burned, with 9% third degree. The patient also sustained second-degree burns of the lower back.

    A. 15100 × 2, T21.62XA, T22.119XA, T31.22

    B. 15100, 15101 × 9, T21.32XA, T21.24XA, T31.20

    C. 15100, 15101 × 9-51, T31.20, T21.32XA, T21.24XA

    D. 15100, 15101 × 8, T21.32XA, T21.24XA, T31.20

33. Libby was thrown from a horse while riding in the ditch; a truck that honked the horn as it passedher startled her horse. The horse reared up, and Libby was thrown to the ground. Her left tibia was fractured and required insertion of multiple pins to stabilize the defect area. A Monticelli multiplane external fixation system was then attached to the pins. Code the placement of the fixation device and-diagnosis only.

A. 20661-LT, V80.21XA, S82.202A, V80.010A, S82.232A, V80.41XA, LT, S82.42XA, V80.41XA

B. S82.221A, 20692-LT, 20692-LT,

C.

D. 20690-

34. A small incision was made over the left proximal tibia, and a traction pin was inserted through thebone to the opposite side. Weights were then affixed to the pins to stabilize the closed tibial fracture temporarily until fracture repair could be performed. Assign codes for the physician service.

A. 20650-LT, S82.102A

B. 20663-LT, S82.142A

C. 20690-LT, S82.231A

D. 20692-LT, S82.156A

35. Mary tells her physician that she has been having pain in her left wrist for several weeks. The physician examines the area and palpates a ganglion cyst of the tendon sheath. He marks the injection sites, sterilizes the area, and injects corticosteroid into two areas.

A. 20550-LT × 2, M67.849
B. 20551-LT, M67.52
C. 20551-LT × 2, M67.469
D. 20612-LT, 20612-59-LT, M67.432

36. The physician applies a Minerva-type fiberglass body cast from the hips to the shoulders and to the head. Before application, a stockinette is stretched over the patient's torso, and further padding of the bony areas with felt padding was done. The patient was diagnosed with Morquio-Brailsford kyphosis. Assign codes for the physician service only.

A. 29040
B. 29590
C. 29025
D. 29000

37. OPERATIVE REPORT

PREOPERATIVE DIAGNOSIS: Compound fracture, left humerus, with possible loss of left radial pulse.

PROCEDURE PERFORMED: Open reduction internal fixation, left compound humerus fracture. PROCEDURE: While under a general anesthetic, the patient's left arm was prepped with Betadine and draped in sterile fashion. We then created a longitudinal incision over the anterolateral aspect of his left arm and carried the dissection through the subcutaneous tissue. We attempted to identify the lateral intermuscular septum and progressed to the fracture site, which was actually fairly easy to do because there was some significant tearing and rupturing of the biceps and brachialis muscles. These were partial ruptures, but the bone was relatively easy to expose through this. We then identified the fracture site and thoroughly irrigated it with several liters of saline. We also noted that the radial nerve was easily visible, crossing along the posterolateral aspect of the fracture site. It was intact. We carefully detected it throughout the remainder of the procedure. We then were able to strip the periosteum away from the lateral side of the shaft of the humerus both proximally and distally from the fracture site. We did this just enough to apply a 6-hole plate, which we eventually held in place with six cortical screws. We did attempt to compress the fracture site. Due to some comminution, the fracture was not quite anatomically aligned, but certainly it was felt to be very acceptable.

Once we had applied the plate, we then checked the radial pulse with a Doppler. We found that theradial pulse was present using the Doppler, but not with palpation. We then applied Xeroform dressings to the wounds and the incision. After padding the arm thoroughly, we applied a long-arm splint with the elbow flexed about 75 degrees. He tolerated the procedure well, and the radial pulsewas again present on Doppler examination at the end of the procedure.

A. 24515-RT
B. 24500-LT
C. 24515-LT
D. 24505-LT

38. OPERATIVE REPORT

PREOPERATIVE DIAGNOSIS: Left thigh abscess.

PROCEDURE PERFORMED: Incision and drainage of left thigh abscess.

OPERATIVE NOTE: With the patient under general anesthesia, he was placed in the lithotomy position. The area around the anus was carefully inspected, and we saw no evidence of communication with the perirectal space. This appears to have risen in the crease at the top of the leg, extending from the posterior buttocks region up toward the side of the base of the penis. In any event, the area was prepped and draped in a sterile manner. Then we incised the area in fluctuation. We obtained a lot of very foul-smelling, almost stool-like material (it was not stool, but it was brown and very foul-smelling material). This was not the typical pus one sees with a Staphylococcus aureus–typeinfection. The incision was widened to allow us to probe the cavity fully. Again, I could see no evidence of communication to the rectum, but there was extension down the thigh and extension up into the groin crease. The fascia was darkened from the purulent material. I opened some of the fasciato make sure the underlying muscle was viable. This appeared viable. No gas was present. There was nothing to suggest a necrotizing fasciitis. The patient did have a very extensive inflammation within this abscess cavity. The abscess cavity was irrigated with peroxide and saline and packed with gauze vaginal packing. The patient tolerated the procedure well and was discharged from the operating roomin stable condition.

A. 26990-LT, L03.119
B. 27301-LT, L02.416
C. 27301-LT, L02.419
D. 27025-LT, L03.229

39. OPERATIVE REPORT

Code only the operative procedure and diagnosis(es). PREOPERATIVE DIAGNOSIS:

1. Hypoxia.
2. Pneumothorax. POSTOPERATIVE DIAGNOSIS:
1. Hypoxia.
2. Pneumothorax.

PROCEDURE: Chest tube placement.

DESCRIPTION OF PROCEDURE: The patient was previously sedated with Versed and paralyzed with Nimbex. Lidocaine was used to numb the incision area in the midlateral left chest at about nipple level. After the lidocaine, an incision was made, and we bluntly dissected to the area of the pleural space, making sure we were superior to the rib. On entrance to the pleural space, there was immediaterelease of air noted. An 18-gauge chest tube was subsequently placed and sutured to the skin. There were no complications for the procedure, and blood loss was minimal.

DISPOSITION: Follow-up, single-view, chest x-ray showed significant resolution of the pneumothorax except for a small apical pneumothorax that was noted.

A. 32422, J94.2, R04.81
B. 32551, J92.9, R09.02
C. 32551, J93.9, R09.02
D. 32422, J93.81, R07.2

40. OPERATIVE PROCEDURE

PREOPERATIVE DIAGNOSIS: 68-year-old male in a coma. POSTOPERATIVE DIAGNOSIS: 68-year-old male in a coma.

PROCEDURE PERFORMED: Placement of a triple lumen central line in right subclavian vein. Withthe usual Betadine scrub to the right subclavian vein area and with a second attempt, the subclavian vein was cannulated and the wire was threaded. The first time the wire did not thread right, and so the attempt was aborted to make sure we had good identification of structures. Once the wire was in place, the needle was removed and a tissue dilator was pushed into position over the wire. Once that was removed, then the central lumen catheter was pushed into position at 17 cm and the wire removed. All three ports were flushed. The catheter was sewn into position, and a dressing applied.

A. 36011, R40.0
B. 36011, R40.1
C. 36556, R40.24
D. 36556, R40.20

41. OPERATIVE REPORT: The patient is in for a bone marrow biopsy. The patient was sterilized bystandard procedure. Bone

marrow core biopsies were obtained from the left posterior iliac crest with minimal discomfort. At the end of the procedure, the patient denied discomfort, without evidence of complications. The patient has diffuse, malignant lymphoma. Assign codes for the physician service only.

A. 20225, C83.70
B. 38221, C83.50
C. 38230, C83.50
D. 38220, C84.17

42. What CPT and ICD-10-CM codes report a percutaneous insertion of a dual-chamber pacemaker by means of the subclavian vein? The diagnosis was sick sinus syndrome, tachy-brady.

A. 33249, I50.1
B. 33217, I49.5
C. 33208, I49.5
D. 33240, I47.2

43. Patient is a 40-year-old male who was involved in a motor vehicle crash. He is having some pulmonary insufficiency.

PROCEDURE: Bronchoscope was inserted through the accessory point on the end of the ET tube andwas then advanced through the ET tube. The ET tube came pretty close down to the carina. We selectively intubated the right mainstem bronchus with the bronchoscope. There were some secretions here, and these were aspirated. We then advanced this selectively into first the lower and then the middle and upper lobes. Secretions were present, more so in the middle and lower lobes. No mucous plug was identified. We then went into the left mainstem and looked at the upper and lower lobes.

There was really not much in the way of secretions present. We did inject some saline and aspirated this out. We then removed the bronchoscope and put the patient back on the supplemental O2. We waited a few minutes. The oxygen level actually stayed pretty good during this time. We then reinserted the bronchoscope and went down to the right side again. We aspirated out all secretions andmade sure everything was clear. We then removed the bronchoscope and pulled back on the ET tube about 1.5 cm. We then again placed the patient on supplemental oxygenation.

FINDINGS: No mucous plug was identified. Secretions were found mainly in the right lung and wereaspirated. The left side looked pretty clear.

    A. 31646, J91.8, Y38.2
    B. 32654, J95.89, Y38.2
    C. 31645-50, J95.2, Y38.2
    D. 31645-RT, J98.4, Y38.2

CPC EXAM PRACTICE 2022

44. This 52-year-old male has undergone several attempts at extubation, all of which failed. He also has morbid obesity and significant subcutaneous fat in his neck. The patient is now in for a flap tracheostomy and cervical lipectomy. The cervical lipectomy is necessary for adequate exposure and access to the trachea and also to secure tracheotomy tube placement. Assign code(s) for the physician service only.

A. 31610, 15839-51
B. 31610
C. 31610, 15838
D. 31603, 15839-5

45. The physician is using an abdominal approach to perform a proctopexy combined with a sigmoidresection; the patient was diagnosed with colon cancer, primary site sigmoid flexure of the colon.
A. 45540, C18.7, C80.0
B. 45541, C18.2, C80.0
C. 45550, C18.7, C79.9
D. 45342, C05.0, C79.9

46. OPERATIVE REPORT

PREOPERATIVE DIAGNOSIS: Abdominal pain POSTOPERATIVE

DIAGNOSIS: Normal endoscopy.

PROCEDURE: The video therapeutic endoscope was passed without difficulty into the oropharynx. The gastroesophageal junction was seen at 40 cm. Inspection of the esophagus revealed no erythema, ulceration, varices, or other mucosal abnormalities. The stomach was entered and the endoscope advanced to the second duodenum. Inspection of the second duodenum, first duodenum, duodenal bulb, and pylorus revealed no abnormalities. Retroflexion revealed no lesions along the curvature.

Inspection of the antrum, body, and fundus of the stomach revealed no abnormalities. The patient tolerated the procedure well. The patient complained of abdominal pain and weight loss.

A. 45378, R10.33
B. 43235, R10.9, R63.4
C. 49320, R63.4
D. 43255, R10.827, R63.

47. This 70-year-old male is brought to the operating room for a biopsy of the pancreas. A wedgebiopsy is taken and sent to pathology. The report comes back immediately indicating that primarymalignant cells were present in the specimen. The decision was made to perform a total pancreatectomy. Code the operative procedure(s) and diagnosis only.

A. 48100-57, C32.3
B. 48155, C26.0
C. 48155, 48100-51, C25.9
D. 48155, 48100-51, 88309, C25.9

48. The patient was taken to the operating room for a repair of a strangulated inguinal hernia. This hernia was previously repaired 4 months ago.

A. 49521, K40.40
B. 49520, K40.11
C. 49492, K40.10
D. 49521-78, K41.30

49. This 43-year-old female comes in with a peritonsillar abscess. The patient is brought to same-daysurgery and given general anesthetic. On examination of the peritonsillar abscess, an incision was made and fluid was drained. The area was examined again, saline was applied, and then the area waspacked with gauze. The patient tolerated the procedure well.

A. 42825, J36
B. 42700, J36
C. 42825, J32.4
D. 42700, J31.1

50. What code would you use to report a rigid proctosigmoidoscopy with removal of two non-adenomatous

polyps of the rectum by snare technique?
A. 45320, K63.1
B. 45384, K61.2
C. 45309 × 2, K62.1
D. 45315, K62.1

51. OPERATIVE REPORT

PREOPERATIVE DIAGNOSIS: Missed abortion with fetal demise, 11 weeks. POSTOPERATIVEDIAGNOSIS: Missed abortion with fetal demise, 11 weeks. PROCEDURE: Suction D&C.

The patient was prepped and draped in a lithotomy position under general mask anesthesia, and the bladder was straight catheterized; a weighted speculum was placed in the vagina. The anterior lip of the cervix was grasped with a single-tooth tenaculum. The uterus was then sounded to a depth of 8 cm. The cervical os was then serially dilated to allow passage of a size 10 curved suction curette. A size 10 curved suction curette was then used to evacuate the intrauterine contents. Sharp curette was used to gently palpate the uterine wall with negative return of tissue, and the suction curette was againused with negative return of tissue. The tenaculum was removed from the cervix. The speculum was removed from the vagina. All sponges and needles were accounted for at completion of the procedure. The patient left the operating room in apparent good condition having tolerated the procedure well.

A. 59812, O03.9
B. 59812, O03.2
C. 59820, O02.1
D. 59856, O02.1

52. OPERATIVE REPORT

PREOPERATIVE DIAGNOSIS: Right ureteral stricture. POSTOPERATIVE DIAGNOSIS: Right ureteral stricture. PROCEDURE PERFORMED: Cystoscopy, right ureteral stent change.

PROCEDURE NOTE: The patient was placed in the lithotomy position after receiving IV sedation. He was prepped and draped in the lithotomy position. The 21-French cystoscope was passed into the bladder, and urine was collected for culture. Inspection of the bladder demonstrated findings consistent with radiation cystitis, which has been previously diagnosed. There is no frank neoplasia. The right ureteral stent was grasped and removed through the urethral meatus; under fluoroscopic control, a guidewire was advanced up the stent, and the stent was exchanged for a 7-French 26-cm stent under fluoroscopic control in the usual fashion. The patient tolerated the procedure well.

A. 51702-LT, N13.5
B. 52005-RT, N22
C. 52332-RT, N21.1
D. 52332-RT, N13.5

53. This patient is a 42-year-old female who has been having prolonged and heavy bleeding duringmenstruation. SURGICAL FINDINGS: On pelvic exam under anesthesia, the uterus was normal size and firm. Theexamination revealed no masses. She had a few small endometrial polyps in the lower uterine segment.

DESCRIPTION OF PROCEDURE: After induction of general anesthesia, the patient was placed in the dorsolithotomy position, after which the perineum and vagina were prepped, the bladder straight catheterized, and the patient draped. After bimanual exam was performed, a weighted speculum was placed in the vagina and the anterior lip of the cervix was grasped with a single toothed tenaculum. An endocervical curettage was then done with a Kevorkian curet. The uterus was then sounded to 8.5 cm. The endocervical canal was dilated to 7 mm with Hegar dilators. A 5.5-mm Olympus hysteroscope was introduced using a distention medium. The cavity was systematically inspected, andthe preceding findings noted. The hysteroscope was withdrawn and the cervix further dilated to 10 mm. Polyp forceps was introduced, and a few small polyps were removed. These were sent separately. Sharp endometrial curettage was then done. The hysteroscope was then reinserted, and the polyps had essentially been removed. The patient tolerated the procedure well and returned to the recovery room in stable condition. Pathology confirmed benign endometrial polyps.

   A. 58558, 57460-51, N82.5, N92.3
   B. 58558, N92.0, N84.0
   C. 58558, 57558-51, N84.1, N92.1
   D. 58558, N92.0, N84.0

54. This patient is 35 years old at 35 weeks' gestation. She presented in spontaneous labor. Because of her prior cesarean section, she is taken to the operating room to have a repeat lower-segment transverse cesarean section performed. The patient also desires sterilization, and so a bilateral tubal ligation will also be performed. A single, liveborn infant was the outcome of the delivery.

A. 59510, 58600-51, Z30.2
B. 59620, 58611, O60.14X0, Z37.0
C. 59514, 58605-51, Z37.0, O60.14X0
D. 59514, 58611, O60.14X0, O34.21, Z37.0, Z30.2

55. OPERATIVE REPORT

PREOPERATIVE DIAGNOSIS: Possible recurrent transitional cell carcinoma of the bladder. POSTOPERATIVE DIAGNOSIS: No evidence of recurrence.

PROCEDURE PERFORMED: Cystoscopy with multiple bladder biopsies.

PROCEDURE NOTE: The patient was given a general mask anesthetic, prepped, and draped in the lithotomy position. The 21-French cystoscope was passed into the bladder. There was a hyperemic area on the posterior wall of the bladder, and a biopsy was taken. Random biopsies of the bladder were also performed. This area was fulgurated. A total of 7 sq cm of bladder was fulgurated. A catheter was left at the end of the procedure. The patient tolerated the procedure well and was transferred to the recovery room in good condition. The pathology report indicated no evidence of recurrence.

A. 52224, Z85.51
B. 51020, 52204, Z80.52
C. 52234, D41.4, Z85.51
D. 52224 × 4, D41.4

56. This 41-year-old female presented with a right labial lesion. A biopsy was taken, and the results were reported as VIN III, cannot rule out invasion. The decision was therefore made to proceed withwide local excision of the right vulva. PROCEDURE: The patient was taken to the operating room, and general anesthesia was administered. The patient was then prepped and draped in the usual manner in lithotomy position, andthe bladder was emptied with a straight catheter. The vulva was then inspected. On the right labium minora at approximately the 11 o'clock position, there was a multifocal lesion. A marking pen was then used to mark out an elliptical incision, leaving a 1-cm border on all sides. The skin ellipse was then excised using a knife. Bleeders were cauterized with electrocautery. A running locked suture of 2-0 Vicryl was then placed in the deeper tissue. The skin was finally reapproximated with 4-0 Vicryl in an interrupted fashion. Good hemostasis was thereby achieved. The patient tolerated this procedurewell. There were no complications.

A. 56605, C51.9   B. 56625, D07.1
C. 56620, D07.1   D. 11620, C50.8

57. OPERATIVE REPORT
PREOPERATIVE DIAGNOSIS: Brain tumor versus abscess.PROCEDURE: Craniotomy.
DESCRIPTION OF PROCEDURE: Under general anesthesia, the patient's head was prepped and draped in the usual manner. It was placed in Mayfield pins. We then proceeded with a craniotomy. An inverted U-shaped incision was made over the poster-

ior right occipital area. The flap was turned down. Three burr holes were made. Having done this, I then localized the tumor through the burr holes and dura. We then made an incision in the dura in an inverted U-shaped fashion. The cortex looked a little swollen but normal. We then used the localizer to locate the cavity. I separated the gyrus and got right into the cavity and saw pus, which was removed. Cultures were taken and sent for pathology report, which came back later describing the presence of clusters of gram-positive cocci, confirming that this was an abscess. We cleaned out the abscessed cavity using irrigation and suction. The bed of the abscessed cavity was cauterized. Then a small piece of Gelfoam was used for hemostasis. Satisfied that it was dry, I closed the dura. I approximated the scalp. A dressing was applied. The patient was discharged to the recovery room.

A. 61154, D49.6
B. 61154, G11.0
C. 61320, G06.0
D. 61150, C24.0

58. This patient came in with an obstructed ventriculoperitoneal shunt. The procedure performed was to be a revision of shunt. After inspecting the shunt system, the entire cerebrospinal fluid shunt system was removed and a similar replacement shunt system was placed. Patient has normal pressure hydrocephalus (NPH).

A. 62180, T85.192D
B. 62258, T85.09XD
C. 62256, T85.09XA
D. 62190, T85.199A

59. This patient is in for a recurrent herniated disc at L5-S1 on the left. The procedure performed is arepeat laminotomy and foraminotomy at the L5-S1 interspace.

A. 63030-LT, M46.45
B. 63030-LT, M30.62
C. 63042-LT, M51.25
D. 63042-LT, M51.27

60. What CPT and ICD-10-CM codes would you assign to report the removal of 30% of the left thyroid lobe, with isthmusectomy? The diagnosis was benign growth of the thy-

roid.

A. 60210, D34
B. 60220, D44.0
C. 60212, D49.7
D. 60225, D44.0, D49.7

61. OPERATIVE REPORT

PREOPERATIVE DIAGNOSIS: Paralytic ectropion, left eye. PROCEDURE PERFORMED: Medial tarsorrhaphy, left eye.

In the operating room, after intravenous sedation, the patient was given a total of about 0.5 mL of local infiltrative anesthetic. The skin surfaces on the medial area of the lid, medial to the punctum, were denuded. A bolster had been prepared and double 5-0 silk suture was passed through the bolster, which was passed through the inferior skin and raw lid margin, then through the superior margin, and out through the skin. A superior bolster was then applied. The puncta were probed with wire instrument and found not to be obstructed. The suture was then fully tied and trimmed. Bacitracin ointment was placed on the surface of the skin. The patient left the operating room in stable condition, without complications, having tolerated the procedure well.

A. 67875-LT, H02.236

B. 67710-LT, H02.129
C. 67882-LT, H02.146
D. 67880-LT, H02.156

62. This 66-year-old male has been diagnosed with a senile cataract of the posterior extracapsular and is scheduled for a cataract extraction by phacoemulsification of the right eye. The physician has taken the patient to the operating room to perform a posterior extracapsular cataract extraction with IOL placement, diffuse of the right eye.

A. 66982-RT
B. 66984-RT

C. 66983-RT   D. 66830-RT

63. Bill, a retired U.S. Air Force pilot, was on observation status 12 hours to assess the outcome of a fall from the back of a parked pickup truck into a gravel pit.

History of Present Illness: The patient is a 42-year-old gentleman who works at the local garden shop. He explained that yesterday he fell from his pickup truck as he was loading gravel for a landscaping project. He lost his footing when attempting to climb from the pickup bed and fell approximately 4 feet and landed on a rock that was protruding from the ground 4 inches, striking his head on the rock. He did not lose consciousness, but was dizzy. He subsequently developed a throbbing headache (8/10) and swelling at the point of impact. The duration of the dizziness was approximately 10 minutes. The headache persisted for 26 hours after the fall. He did take ibuprofen without significant improvement in the pain level. Review of Systems: Constitutional, eyes, ears, nose, throat, lungs, cardiovascular, gastrointestinal, skin, neurologic, lymphatic, and immunologic negative except for HPI statements.

PFSH: He is married and has 2 children. He has been working at the garden shop for 4 years. He currently smokes one pack of cigarettes a day and has smoked for 10 years. His father died of heart disease when he was 52. He has one brother with ankylosing spondylitis and one sister who is healthy as far as he knows. His mother died when he was 14 years old. He is currently on no prescribed medications. A comprehensive exam is documented and rendered. The medical decision making is of low complexity.

The physician discharged Bill from observation that same day after 10 hours, after determining that no further monitoring of his condition was necessary. The physician provided a detailed examination and indicated that the medical decision making was of a low complexity.

A. 99218, W18.39XA, R42   B. 99234, Z04.3,
W17.89XA, R42, R51

C. 99217, W14.XXXA, R51 D. 99234, 99217,
W20.XXA, Z04.3

64. Dr. Martin admits a 65-year-old female patient to the hospital to rule out acute pericarditis following a severe viral infection. The patient has complained of retrosternal, sharp, intermittent pain of 2 days' duration that is reduced by sitting up and leaning forward, accompanied by tachypnea. ROS: She does not currently have chest pain but is complaining of shortness of breath. She states that her legs and feet have been swollen of late. She reports no change in her vision or her hearing, and shehas not had a rash. No dyspnea stated. PFSH: She states that she has had and echocardiogram in the past when she complained of chest tightness and her family physician gave her some medication, but she is not certain what it was. She has three adult children, all healthy. Her husband is deceased. She does not smoke or consume alcohol. Her father died at age 69 from congestive heart failure and her mother died of influenza at 70. Refer to the admission form for a list of current medications. The examination was detailed. The medical decision making was of high complexity.

A. 99236, R06.82, R06.02 B. 99223, I20.0,
K22.9

C. 99245, I20.0, I30.0 D. 99221, R07.2,
R06.82

65. A gynecologist admits an established patient, a 35-year-old female with dysfunctional uterine bleeding, after seeing her in the clinic that day. During the course of the history, the physician notes that the patient has a history of infrequent periods of heavy flow. She has had irregular heavy periods and intermittent spotting for 4 years. The patient has been on a 3-month course of oral contraceptives for symptoms with no relief. The patient states that she has occasional headaches. A complete ROS was performed, consisting of constitutional factors, ophthalmologic, otolaryngologic, cardiovascular, respiratory, gastrointestinal, genitourinary, musculoskeletal, integumentary, neurologic, psychiatric, endocrine,

hematologic, lymphatic, allergic, and immunologic which were all negative, except for the symptoms described above. The family history is positive for endometrial cancer, with mother, two aunts, and two sisters who had endometrial cancer. The patient has a personal history of cervical and endometrial polyp removal 3 years prior to admission. The patients states that she does not smoke andonly drinks socially. As a part of the comprehensive examination, the physician notes the patient has alarge amount of blood in the vault and an enlarged uterus. The prolonged hemorrhaging has resulted in a very thin and friable endometrial lining. The physician orders the patient to be started on intravenous Premarin and orders a full laboratory workup. The medical decision making is of moderate complexity.

A. 99215, 99222, N93.8, Z87.42
B. 99222, N93.8, Z87.42, Z80.49
C. 99215, 99222, N89.8, Z87.42
D. 99222, N91.5, Z80.49

66. Dr. Black admits a patient with an 8-day history of a low-grade fever, tachycardia, tachypnea, and radiologic evidence of basal consolidation of the lung and limited pleural effusion on the left side, per patient as seen at outside clinic several days prior. The patient has also been experiencing swellingof the extremities. The pulse is rapid and thready, as checked by patient on her own during the past couple days. A complete ROS of constitutional factors, ophthalmologic, otolaryngologic, cardiovascular, respiratory, gastrointestinal, genitourinary, musculoskeletal, integumentary, neurologic, psychiatric, endocrine, hematologic, lymphatic, allergic, and immunologic was performed and negative except for the symptoms described above. Past history includes tachycardia and pneumonia. Family history includes heart disease, hypertension and high cholesterol in both parents. The patient drinks only occasionally and quit smoking four years ago. The comprehensive examination was performed and diminished bowel sounds were noted. The physician orders laboratory tests and radiographic studies, including a follow-up chest x-ray as he considers the extensive diagnostic options and the medical decision making complexity is high for this patient.

A. 99234
B. 99213

C. 99236   D. 99223

67. Dr. Stephanopolis makes subsequent hospital visits to Salanda Ortez, who has been in the hospital for primary viral pneumonia. She was experiencing severe dyspnea, rales, fever, and chest pain for over a week. The patient states that this morning she had nausea and her heart was racing while she was experiencing some dyspnea and SOB. The chest radiography showed patchy bilateral infiltrates and basilar streaking. Sputum microbiology was positive for a secondary bacterial pneumonia. An expanded problem-focused physical examination was performed. The medical decision making was moderate. The patient was given intravenous antibiotic as treatment for the bacterial pneumonia.

A. 99233, J15.8, J12.2   B. 99232, J15.9, J12.9
C. 99221, J11.0, J10.82   D. 99234, J14, J15.9

68. A 57-year-old male was sent by his family physician to a urologist for an office consultation dueto hematuria. The patient has had bright red blood in his urine sporadically for the past 3 weeks. His family physician gave him a dose of antibiotic therapy for urinary tract infection; however, the symptom still persists. The patient states that he does experience some lower back discomfort when urinating, with no fever, chills or nausea. The patient is currently taking Lotrel 10/20 for his hypertension which is stable at this time and has allergies to Sulfa. The urologist performs a detailed history and physical examination. The urologist recommends a cystoscopy to be scheduled for the following day and discusses the procedure and risks with the patient. The urologist also contacted the family physician with the recommendations and is requested to proceed with the cystoscopy and any further follow-up required. The medical decision making is of moderate complexity. A report was sent to attending physician. Report only the office service.

A. 99243, R31.9, M54.5
B. 99244-57, 52000, R33, M54.9
C. 99253, R35, M53.2

D. 99221, R39.8, M50.9

69. Which HCPCS modifier indicates an anesthesia service in which the anesthesiologist medically directs one CRNA?
A. QX
B. QY
C. QZ
D. QK

70. Anesthesia service for a pneumocentesis for lung aspiration, 32420.
A. 00522
B. 00500
C. 00520
D. 00524

71. This type of anesthesia is also known as a nerve block.
A. Local
B. Epidural
C. Regional
D. MAC

72. This is the anesthesia formula:
A. B + M + P
B. B + P + M
C. B + T + M
D. B + T + N

73. This 69-year-old female is in for a magnetic resonance examination of the brain because of new seizure activity. After imaging without contrast, contrast was administered and further sequences were performed. Examination results indicated no apparent neoplasm or vascular malformation.
A. 70543-26, R56.00
B. 70543-26, R53.81
C. 70553-26, R56.9
D. 70553, R49.0

74. This patient undergoes a gallbladder sonogram due to epigastric pain. The report indicates that the visualized portions of the liver are normal. No free fluid noted within Morison's pouch. The gallbladder is identified and is empty. No evidence of wall thickening or surrounding fluid is seen. There is no ductal dilatation. The common hepatic duct and common bile duct measure 0.4 and 0.8cm, respectively. The common bile duct measurement is at the upper limits of normal.

A. 76700-26, R10.84
B. 76705-26, R10.13
C. 76775-26, R10.33
D. 76705, R10.81

75. EXAMINATION OF: Chest. CLINICAL SYMPTOMS: Pneumonia. PA AND LATERAL CHEST X-RAY WITH FLUOROSCOPY. CONCLUSION: Ventilation within the lung fields has improved compared with previous study.

A. 71020-26, J15.8
B. 71034, J15.6
C. 71023-26, J18.9
D. 71023, J11.1

76. EXAMINATION OF:
Abdomen and pelvis.
CLINICAL SYMPTOMS:
Ascites.
CT OF ABDOMEN AND PELVIS: Technique: CT of the abdomen and pelvis was performed without oral or IV contrast material per physician request. No previous CT scans for comparison. FINDINGS: No ascites. Moderate-sized pleural effusion on the right.

A. 74176
B. 74176-26
C. 74150, 72192
D. 74177

77. EXAMINATION OF: Brain.
CLINICAL FINDING: Headache.
COMPUTED TOMOGRAPHY OF THE BRAIN was performed without contrast material. FINDINGS: There is blood within the third ventricle. The lateral ventricles show mild dilatation with small amounts of blood.
IMPRESSION:
Acute subarachnoid hemorrhage.

A. 70460-26, G44.1
B. 70250, I74.1
C. 70450, I60.9
D. 70450-26, I73.8

78. Report both the technical and professional components of the following service: This 68 year-old male is seen in Radiation Oncology Department for prostate cancer. The oncologist performs a complex clinical treatment planning, dosimetry calculation, complex isodose plan; treatment devices include blocks, special shields, wedges, and treatment man-

agement. The patient had 5 days of radiation treatments for 2 weeks, a total of 10 days of treatment.

A. 77263, 77300, 77307, 77334, C61

B. 77300, 77307, 77334, 77427 X 2, C61

C. 77263, 77307, 77427 X 2, C61

D. 77263, 77427 X 2, C61

79. CLINICAL HISTORY: Necrotic soleus muscle, right leg. SPECIMEN RECEIVED: Soleus muscle, right leg.

GROSS DESCRIPTION: Submitted in formalin, labeled with the patient's name and "soleus muscle right leg," are multiple irregular fragments of tan, gray, brown soft tissue measuring 8 × 8 × 2.5 cm inaggregate. Multiple representative fragments are submitted in four cassettes.

MICROSCOPIC DESCRIPTION: The slides show multiple sections of skeletal muscle showingsevere coagulative and liquefactive necrosis. Patchy neutrophilic infiltrates are present within thenecrotic tissue.

DIAGNOSIS: Soft tissue, soleus muscle, right leg debridement; necrosis and patchy acuteinflammation, skeletal muscle— infective myositis.

A. 88305-26, M62.50

B. 88304-26, I96

C. 88307-26, I96

D. 88304-26, M46.98

80. This 34-year-old established female patient is in for her yearly physical and lab. The physicianorders a comprehensive metabolic panel, hemogram automated and manual differential WBC count (CBC), and a thyroid-stimulating hormone. Code the lab only.

A. 99395, 80050

B. 80050-52

C. 80069, 80050

D. 80050

81. This is a patient with atrial fibrillation who comes to the clinic laboratory routinely for aquantitative digoxin level. A. 80305, Z46.1, Z82.61, I34.0

B. 80306, Z44.2, Z83.42, I50.3
C. 80162, Z51.81, Z79.899, I48.91
D. 80162, Z41.8, Z80.52, I63.1

82. This patient presented to the laboratory yesterday for a creatine measurement. The results came back at higher than normal levels; therefore, the patient was asked to return to the laboratory today for a repeat creatine test before the nephrologist is consulted. Report the second day of test only.

A. 82540 × 2, R78.89
B. 82550, R79.0
C. 82550, R79.81
D. 82540, R79.89

83. Code a pregnancy test, urine.

A. 84702
B. 84703
C. 81025
D. 84702 × 2

84. What CPT code would you use to code a bilirubin, total (transcutaneous)? A. 82252
B. 82247
C. 82248
D. 88720

85. DIALYSIS INPATIENT NOTE: This 24-year-old male patient is on continuous ambulatory peritoneal dialysis (CAPD) using 1.5%. He drains more than 600 mL. He is tolerating dialysis well. He continues to have some abdominal pain, but his abdomen is not distended. He has some diarrhea. His abdomen does not look like acute abdomen. His vitals, other than blood pressure in the 190s over100s, are fine. He is afebrile.

At this time, I will continue with 1.5% dialysate. I gave him labetalol IV for blood pressure. Becauseof diarrhea, I am going to check stool for white cells, culture. Next we will see what the primary physician says today. His HIDA scan was normal. The patient suffers from ESRD.

A. 90947, 90960, N13.7, R10.3   B. 90945, N18.6, R19.7
C. 90960, N17.2, R19.5   D. 90945, N15.8, R18.8

86. INDICATION: Hypertension with newly diagnosed acute myocardial infarction. PROCEDURE PERFORMED: Insertion of Swan-Ganz catheter.

DESCRIPTION OF PROCEDURE: The right internal jugular and subclavian area was prepped with antiseptic solution. Sterile drapes were applied. Under usual sterile precautions, the right internal jugular vein was cannulated. A 9-French introducer was inserted, and a 7-French Swan-Ganz catheter was inserted without difficulty. Right atrial pressures were 2 to 3, right ventricular pressures 24/0, andpulmonary artery 26/9 with a wedge pressure of 5. This is a Trendelenburg position. The patient tolerated the procedure well.

A. 93501, 93503-51, I26.0, I25.7
B. 93508, I34.0
C. 93503, 93539, I25.9, I30
D. 93503, I21.9, I11.9

87. DIAGNOSIS: Atrial flutter.
PROCEDURE PERFORMED: Electrical cardioversion.
DESCRIPTION OF PROCEDURE: The patient was sedated with Versed and morphine. She wasgiven a total of 5 mg of Versed. She was cardioverted with 50 joules into sinus tachycardia.
The patient was given a 20-mg Cardizem IV push. Her heart rate went down to the 110s, and she wasdefinitely in sinus tachycardia. CONCLUSION: Successful electrical cardioversion of atrial flutter into sinus tachycardia. A. 92961, I49.1   B. 92960, I48.92
C. 92960, 92973, I46.9   D. 92960, I49.8

88. A patient presents for a pleural cavity chemotherapy session with 10 mg doxorubicin HCl thatrequires a thoracentesis to be performed.
A. 96446, J9000
B. 96440, 32554, J9000
C. 96440, J9000
D. 96446, 32554, J9000

89. What CPT code would be used to report a home visit for a respiratory patient to care for themechanical ventilation? A. 99503   B. 99504
C. 99505   D. 99509

90. What CPT code would be used to code the technical aspect of an evaluation of swallowing byvideo recording using a flexible fiberoptic endoscope?
A. 92611   B. 92612
C. 92610   D. 92613

91. A patient saw an Orthopedist on a consultation basis 18 months ago for symptoms of lower back pain. The patient non returns to see the Orthopedist after being referred by his primary care physician again for symptoms of lower back pain. The patient is considered as:

a. New patient
b. Established patient
c. Inpatient
d. Out patient

92. The patient is brought to surgery room for repair of an accidentally inflicted open wound of the left thigh, the total extent measuring approximately 40 x 35 cm. DESCRIPTION OF PROCEDURE: The legs were prepped

with Betadine scrub and solution and then draped in a routine sterile fashion. Split-thickness skin grafts measuring about a 10,000th inch thick were taken from both thighs, meshed with a 3:1 ratio mesher, and stapled to the wounds. The donor sites were dressed with scarlet red, and the recipient sites were dressed with Xeroform, Kerlix fluffs, and Kerlix roll, and a few ABD pads were used for absorption. Estimated blood loss was negligible. The patient tolerated the procedure well and left surgery in good condition.

What type of graft is used for the procedure?

a. Allograft

b. Split thickness graft

c. Autograft

d. None of the above

93. John, an 84-year-old male, tripped while on his morning walk. He stated he was thinking about something else when he inadvertently tripped over the sidewalk curb and fell to his knees. X-ray indicated a comminuted fracture of his right patella. With the patient under general anesthesia, the area was opened and extensively irrigated. The left aspect of the patella was severely fragmented, and a portion of the patella was subsequently removed. The remaining patella fractures were wired. The surrounding tissue was repaired, thoroughly irrigated, and closed in the usual manner.

What type of anesthesia procedure for the operation?

a. General Anesthesia
b. Regional Anesthesia
c. Local anesthesia
d. Sedation

94. PREOPERATIVE DIAGNOSIS: Leaking from intestinal anastomosis.

POSTOPERATIVE DIAGNOSIS: Leaking from intestinal anastomosis. PROCEDURE PERFORMED: Proximal ileostomy for diversion of colon. Overview of right colonic fistula.

OPERATIVE NOTE: This patient was taken back to the operating room from the intensive care unit. She was having acute signs of leakage from an anastomosis I performed 3 days previously. We took down some of the sutures holding the wound together. We basically exposed all of this patient's intestine. It was evident that she was leaking from the small bowel as well as from the right colon. I thought the only thing we could do would be to repair the right colon. This was done in two layers, and then we freed up enough bowel to try to make an ileostomy proximal to the area of leakage. We were able to do this with great difficulty, and there was only a small amount of bowel to be brought out. We brought this out as an ileostomy stoma, realizing that it was of questionable viability and that it should be watched closely. With that accomplished, we then packed the wound and returned the patient to the intensive care unit.

For colon diversion the doctor performed?

a. Proximal ileostomy
b. Colonoscopy
c. Deodenectomy
d. Esophageal hiatus

> 95. OPERATIVE REPORT PREOPERATIVE DIAGNOSIS: Fever of unknown origin PROCEDURE PERFORMED: Lumbar puncture.

DESCRIPTION OF PROCEDURE: The patient was placed in the lateral decubitus position with the left side up. The legs and hips were flexed into the fetal position. The lumbosacral area was sterilely prepped. It was then numbed with 1% Xylocaine. I then placed a 22-gauge spinal needle on the first pass into the intrathecal space between the LA and L5 spinous processes. The fluid was minimally xanthochromic I sent the fluid for cell count for differential, protein, glucose, Gram stain, and culture. The patient tolerated the procedure well without apparent complication. The needle was removed at the end of the procedure. The area was cleansed, and a Band-Aid was placed.

In which area was sterile prepped?

a. Thoraco cavity
b. Lumbo sacral
c. Supine position
d. Lamellar region

> 96. A 32-year old woman complained of irritation and deposits on the eyelids. Visualization by slit lamp revealed multiple eggs attached to eyelashes and a mobile foreign body. What is the diagnosis?

a. Preorbital cellulitis
b. Blepharitis
Pediculosis d.Chalazion

97. A 51-year old patient with a history of type 2 diabetes presented with brown-to-black, poorly defined, velvety hyper-pigmentation of the skin. Can you name the medical sign?
a. Keratosis nigricans
b. Cyanosis
c. Vitiligo
d. None of these

98. A 47-year old male with no significant past medical history presents to the office complaining of a new rash in his armpits. He first noticed it 1 month ago, and since then it has grown "darker, thicker, and larger". He reports that it is occasionally mildly pruritic. His vital signs are normal. Upon examination he has hyper-pigmented tick plaque in both axillae. Which of the following is the most appropriate laboratory test to order?
a. Thyroid stimulating hormone
b. Fasting blood glucose
c. Fasting lipid panel
d. Serum electrolytes

99. A child was born with the failure of the spine to close over into a proper canal. The lump is a combination of nerves and skin exposed to the air. The baby's spinal cord fails to develop properly. This birth defect is known as
a. Spina bifida
b. Lordosis
c. Kyphosis
d. Scoliosis

100. A neurological consultation in the emergency department of the local hospital is requested by the ED physician for a 25-year-old male with suspected closed head trauma. The neurologist saw the patient in the ED. The patient had a loss of consciousness this morning after receiving a blow to the head in a basketball game. He presents to the emergency department with a headache, dizziness, and confusion During the course of the history, the patient relates that he has been very irritable, confused, and has had a bit of nausea since the incident. All other systems reviewed and are negative: Constitutional, ophthalmologic, otolaryngologic, cardiovascular, respiratory, genitourinary, musculoskeletal, integumentary, psychiatric, endocrine, hematologic, lymphatic, allergic, and immunologic. The patients states that he does have a history of headaches and that both parents have hypertension, also a grandfather with heart disease. He also states that he does drink beer on the weekends and does not smoke. Physical examination reveals the patient to be unsteady and exhibiting difficulty in concentration when stating months in reverse. The pupils dilate unequally. The physician continues with a complete comprehensive examination involving an extensive review of neurological function. The neurologist orders a stat CT and MRI. The physician suspects a subdural hematoma or an epidural hematoma and the medical decision-making complexity is high. The neurologist admits the patient to the hospital. Assign codes for the neurologist's services only. Which radiology tests are ordered by the neurologist?

a. Comprehensive Testing and Memory Resonance imaging
b. Computed tomography and Magnetic Resonance Imaging
c. Continues Testing and Micro Resonance Imaging
d. Compress Testing and Mini Resonance Imaging

ANSWERS

EXAM – 1 ANSWERS

1	C	21	C	41	C	61	A	81	C
2	A	22	B	42	D	62	D	82	C
3	B	23	A	43	A	63	C	83	B
4	A	24	C	44	D	64	D	84	D
5	C	25	A	45	B	65	D	85	D
6	D	26	A	46	C	66	A	86	A
7	A	27	C	47	A	67	A	87	D
8	A	28	A	48	A	68	B	88	C
9	B	29	B	49	D	69	C	89	D
10	B	30	B	50	A	70	A	90	B
11	C	31	A	51	B	71	D	91	C
12	A	32	D	52	B	72	B	92	D
13	A	33	D	53	D	73	A	93	D
14	A	34	D	54	A	74	A	94	D
15	B	35	C	55	B	75	B	95	B
16	D	36	B	56	D	76	D	96	D
17	C	37	B	57	A	77	D	97	D
18	A	38	C	58	C	78	A	98	C
19	B	39	C	59	A	79	D	99	B
20	A	40	A	60	B	80	C	100	B

EXAM – 2 ANSWERS

1. c	21. a	41. d	61. d	81. a
2. d	22. b	42. a	62. c	82. a
3. c	23. b	43. b	63. a	83. c
4. d	24. d	44. a	64. c	84. d
5. d	25. d	45. d	65. a	85. a
6. b	26. a	46. c	66. b	86. a
7. d	27. c	47. d	67. b	87. d
8. b	28. d	48. d	68. d	88. a
9. a	29. b	49. a	69. b	89. c
10. a	30. b	50. d	70. b	90. b
11. b	31. b	51. b	71. d	91. c
12. c	32. b	52. a	72. a	92. c
13. b	33. b	53. d	73. b	93. c
14. b	34. d	54. c	74. c	94. b
15. b	35. b	55. d	75. b	95. b
16. b	36. b	56. b	76. c	96. b

17. b	37. a	57. c	77. c	97. a
18. d	38. d	58. a	78. d	98. b
19. a	39. a	59. d	79. a	99. c
20. a	40. a	60. a	80. b	100. b

EXAM - 3 ANSWERS

1	D	26	B	51	D	76	A
2	A	27	A	52	A	77	C
3	D	28	A	53	B	78	C
4	C	29	C	54	A	79	A
5	B	30	D	55	A	80	A
6	B	31	A	56	C	81	A
7	A	32	D	57	D	82	B
8	A	33	B	58	C	83	B
9	D	34	A	59	A	84	B
10	B	35	D	60	B	85	D
11	C	36	A	61	C	86	B
12	B	37	B	62	D	87	D
13	A	38	D	63	B	88	C
14	B	39	A	64	A	89	C
15	A	40	C	65	B	90	C
16	D	41	B	66	A	91	A
17	C	42	D	67	B	92	B
18	A	43	B	68	D	93	A
19	B	44	C	69	A	94	B
20	D	45	D	70	C	95	C
21	D	46	B	71	A	96	A
22	A	47	A	72	D	97	B
23	C	48	C	73	B	98	D

| 24 | A | 49 | B | 74 | B | 99 | C |
| 25 | C | 50 | B | 75 | C | 100 | A |

EXAM - 4 ANSWERS

1	C	21	A	41	C	61	B	81	A
2	B	22	B	42	C	62	B	82	D
3	A	23	D	43	D	63	B	83	B
4	D	24	C	44	A	64	B	84	C
5	D	25	D	45	A	65	B	85	A
6	C	26	A	46	C	66	D	86	B
7	B	27	B	47	A	67	A	87	C
8	C	28	C	48	D	68	A	88	C
9	A	29	A	49	B	69	B	89	C
10	D	30	A	50	A	70	C	90	A
11	B	31	A	51	D	71	D		
12	B	32	B	52	A	72	B		
13	A	33	A	53	C	73	C		
14	A	34	D	54	B	74	A		
15	D	35	A	55	B	75	D		
16	A	36	B	56	B	76	D		
17	D	37	A	57	B	77	B		
18	C	38	A	58	A	78	D		
19	B	39	A	59	C	79	A		
20	B	40	B	60	A	80	C		

91. 17311, 17312, 17315, 12002

92. 14020, C44.42

93. 15120-58, 15004-58, E11.621, L97.509

94. 17311, 13152-51, C44119

95. 29819

96. 19081

97. 12011, S01.21XA, W18.49XA

98. 44310-78

99. 62270

100. 11406, 12032, D21.6

EXAM – 5 ANSWERS

1	C	21	B	41	D	61	A	81	C
2	D	22	C	42	B	62	D	82	B
3	D	23	C	43	C	63	D	83	B
4	C	24	B	44	B	64	C	84	A
5	B	25	A	45	D	65	D	85	D
6	B	26	B	46	B	66	C	86	D
7	C	27	B	47	C	67	C	87	C
8	A	28	C	48	B	68	D	88	A
9	D	29	A	49	A	69	D	89	B
10	D	30	D	50	C	70	B	90	B
11	C	31	B	51	A	71	B	91	B
12	C	32	B	52	D	72	C	92	B
13	A	33	C	53	B	73	C	93	A
14	D	34	C	54	D	74	D	94	D
15	D	35	C	55	C	75	C	95	A
16	C	36	D	56	B	76	C	96	C
17	A	37	C	57	B	77	D	97	B
18	B	38	B	58	D	78	D	98	C
19	C	39	A	59	D	79	A	99	B
20	D	40	B	60	C	80	A	100	B

EXAM – 6 ANSWERS

#	Ans	#	Ans	#	Ans	#	Ans
1	D	26	D	51	C	76	B
2	A	27	C	52	D	77	C
3	B	28	B	53	B	78	C
4	D	29	D	54	D	79	B
5	C	30	D	55	A	80	D
6	A	31	C	56	C	81	C
7	A	32	B	57	C	82	D
8	D	33	B	58	B	83	C
9	C	34	A	59	D	84	B
10	A	35	D	60	A	85	C
11	B	36	A	61	D	86	D
12	B	37	C	62	B	87	B
13	D	38	B	63	B	88	C
14	D	39	C	64	D	89	B
15	D	40	D	65	B	90	B
16	D	41	B	66	D	91	B
17	C	42	C	67	B	92	B
18	A	43	D	68	B	93	A
19	B	44	A	69	B	94	A
20	C	45	C	70	D	95	B
21	C	46	B	71	A	96	C
22	D	47	C	72	C	97	A
23	B	48	A	73	C	98	B

24	C	49	B	74	B	99	A
25	B	50	D	75	C	100	B

Thank you

Made in the USA
Las Vegas, NV
07 March 2023